'A Guest is a Gift from God'

With best wishes

From Vivian McTear

AKA Conor Mc Keen

March 2013

For my wife Linda and children Annalies and Daniel,
who are, and will always be, the light of my life.

'A guest is a gift from God'
Travels in Georgia

Conor McKeever

GREEN PRINT

© Conor McKeever, 2012

Published in the UK in 2012 by Green Print
an imprint of
The Merlin Press Ltd
6 Crane Street Chambers
Crane Street
Pontypool
NP4 6ND
Wales
www.merlinpress.co.uk

ISBN. 978-1-85425-100-8

British Library Cataloguing in Publication Data is available from the
British Library

Printed in the UK by Imprint Digital, Exeter

CONTENTS

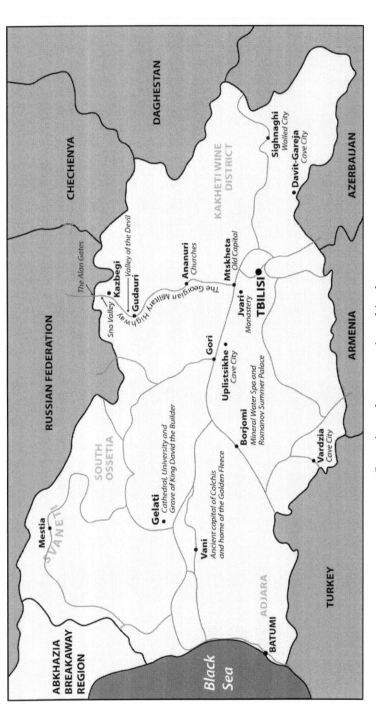

Georgia – places mentioned in the text

Illlustrations between pages 88 and 89

Examples of Georgia's artistic legacy dating from the 4th millennium BC exhibited in the various Museums and Galleries which comprise the Georgian National Museum.

Plate 1. Gold earrings, fourth century BC. Janashia Museum of Georgia, Tbilisi: Georgian National Museum.

Plate 2. Gold brooch with garnets. Vani, fourth century BC. Janashia Museum of Georgia, Tbilisi: Georgian National Museum.

Plate 3. Gold necklace with turtles. Vani, fifth century BC. Janashia Museum of Georgia, Tbilisi: Georgian National Museum.

Plate 3a. Detail of above.

Plate 4. Gold ornaments for horse's harness, fourth century BC. Janashia Museum of Georgia, Tbilisi: Georgian National Museum.

Plate 5. Gold lion from a funeral chariot. third millennium BC.

Plate 6. Gold bowl with inlaid cornelian, lapis lazuli & amber. 2000- 1500 BC. Janashia Museum of Georgia, Tbilisi: Georgian National Museum.

Plate 7. Gold earrings with horsemen, Vani, fourth century BC . Janashia Museum of Georgia, Tbilisi: Georgian National Museum.

Plate 8. Icon of St George. Gold, cloisonné enamels, Art Museum of Georgia, Tbilisi: Georgian National Museum

Plate 9. Pectoral Cross of Queen Tamara, late twelfth to early thirteenth centuries. Art Museum of Georgia, Tbilisi: Georgian National Museum.

Plate 10. Our Lady of Khakhuli triptych, eleventh century.

Plates 10a & 10b. details of above.

Preface

In 2005, I was surprised and privileged to find myself working as a consultant in the Republic of Georgia in the Caucasus Mountain between the Black Sea and the Caspian. I found there a country recently liberated from Russian domination, determined to assert its independence and keen to engage with the West but equally determined to do so on its own terms, and in its own unique time-honoured way.

I confess that I quickly fell in love with Georgia and its warm-hearted people, especially those with whom I served during my stay. So much so that I could not resist writing about my adventures to try to engage people everywhere in my love affair with Georgia, and encourage them to undertake their own adventure by visiting this little known enchantress tucked away in the mysterious and beautiful Caucasus. And how could the delightful people with whom I served, and who so generously lived up to the age-old Georgian maxim that 'A Guest is a Gift from God', not take pride-of-place in my story though, to spare their blushes, I have taken liberties with all of their names. Even so, if I have offended in any way in telling my story, I apologise at the outset, and as Shakespeare would have it 'Humbly do beseech you of your pardon...'

So let me introduce, with respect and affection, Tamuna who gently but firmly kept us all in check, even if she sometimes had to resort to the elusive Soso to keep us in line; and the graceful Nana and spirited Eka who took turns at inducting me into the skill of multi-tasking, 'Supra' feasting, and great great wines; to my drivers and minders, Lado ,the 'supra thrower' par excellence, and Andreo, he of the mobile phone and tortuous love-life, and to the many and various loves also of that other great Nimrod of the open road, Yorkshire Pete. Then there is Manana and Andreo who welcomed Jesus and me to their home that Christmas night, the Presidential guards, Kote and Ilia, who I proudly led astray with good Irish whiskey, and the venerable Marlen, high up in the enchanting land of the Svans, who might be 104 years old... or maybe 108! Last but far from least let me introduce the two American members of the team, robust Mitch and earnest Frank who were so generous with their knowledge, skill and time, and who, whatever our trials and triumphs, were unfailingly great 'craic' to be with, surely the highest of Irish accolades! These are just some of the friends and colleagues in this account of my sojourn in Georgia as we engaged in intensive work tempered by visits to Cave Cities on Silk Roads, pursued Jason and the Golden Fleece, attended to sick cows on the frontiers of Russia and walked, at their request, on the bodies of long dead Georgian kings.

Conor McKeever
Belfast 2012

Introduction

'Georgia on my mind'

This is a very personal account of living and working in a small country tucked away in a fold of the Caucasus Mountains on the borders of Asia. The country is Georgia, and in many ways it is a mirror image of my homeland, Northern Ireland. Both are beautiful countries with warm hearted generous people but too often they have hit the world headlines for all the wrong reasons. Over past years, a bemused world has watched nightly on its TV screens refugees fleeing from their blazing homes, angry men and women confronting soldiers, weeping children, claim and counter claim, both countries in turmoil. Peace of a kind has finally descended on Georgia and Northern Ireland but it is an uneasy peace, and there are still occasional images on the TV screens of fresh trouble brewing only just contained beneath a surface of fragile peace.

But this story is about a much happier Georgia as I encountered it a few short years ago when I worked there. That

Georgia was recovering from centuries of oppression and neglect and was hopeful for its future. Its people were welcoming, and working hard to restore their country to its former prosperity. They were keen – perhaps too keen – to embrace the West in every sense, but careful also to cherish their own distinct culture and way of life. Georgians have suffered much over their long history. Tbilisi, their capital, has been literally wiped off the map by invaders over forty times. But despite their problems, past and present, their pride in their country and passion for life is undiminished. Like the Irish, they have eaten and drunk, danced and sung their way down through centuries of triumph and tribulation. Despite recent difficulties, they are keen to let the West know that an independent free Georgia is once again 'open for business'.

Georgia is an enchanting land, its scenery is breathtaking. Few places on earth can match the snow covered High Caucasus that separate Georgia from Russia in the north, and that contrasts with the gentler valleys and exuberant rivers of the Lesser Caucasus marking its southern border with Turkey. To the west is the spectacular Black Sea coast, and to the east, where Georgia merges with Azerbaijan and Armenia, there is the beautiful stark semi-desert landscape tailor-made for poetry and contemplation.

Then there is Georgia's farming land and the variety of its crops – potatoes growing under vines, tea growing among strawberries, pomegranates with kiwi fruit, orchards of apples, pears, peaches, oranges, and groves of walnut and plum trees. All rich and lush and natural with hardly an artificial fertiliser in sight. No wonder Georgia produces some of the most healthy and delicious food in the world.

Georgia's colourful history can match our own for, like Northern Ireland, it has long been a disputed land. It has always been a major crossroads between east and west, north and south. As a result, nearly every invader you can think of – Greeks, Romans, Persians, Byzantines, Arabs, Mongols, Turks, and Russians – have been there wreaking havoc, and none more so than Georgia's very own Comrade Stalin.

Joseph Stalin – a native son of Georgia

So far, Georgia has survived them all, with its own ancient form of Orthodox Christianity, its beautiful vibrant language, distinct culinary tradition, and rich culture totally intact. Georgia's Golden Age was in the twelfth century when it was ruled by King David the Builder and then by Queen Tamara, both of whom left such an indelible mark on the country that, despite their best efforts, even the savage Genghis Khan and Tamerlane could not entirely destroy that regal heritage.

But Georgia is still a disputed land. When Soviet control of the country collapsed in 1991, Georgia declared its independence from Russia, but the Russians are reluctant to give up such a fine jewel, and are constantly trying to get Georgia back under their influence. Then there is the lure of oil that the West finds irresistible; the place is now awash with oilmen and businessmen of all hues. The oil pipeline linking the Caspian to the Black Sea runs right through Georgia, and the West wants to control that oil. No surprise then that even American Presidents take time out to visit Georgia, and Russian tanks roll down its mountain passes to take up commanding positions at the country's very heart.

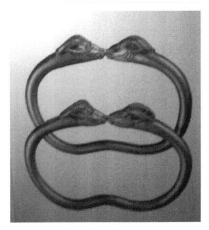

Gold bracelets, fourth century BC, Vani, Georgia

There are still more ancient Georgian treasures: museums packed with exquisite jewellery dating from the time of Jason and the Golden Fleece, priceless icons dating almost to the time of Christ, the natural hot baths in the old city of Tbilisi where, over two thousand and more years, folk have refreshed themselves – from Alexander the Great to George Bush Junior. And you can ponder on how a man can be a hero for some and a tyrant for others when you visit Stalin's birthplace in the city of Gori in central Georgia. You can be renewed by taking the spa waters at beautiful Borjomi, journey up the nerve-racking highway to the magnificent land of the Svan people high in the Caucasus or take that other great mountain adventure, the Georgian Military Highway to the borders of Russia. You can follow in Marco Polo's footsteps along the ancient Silk Road which runs through Georgia and once linked Constantinople to China, and explore the great Cave Cities that guarded the Silk Road. All that and much more is to be found in the land of poetry that is Georgia.

But whatever you make of all these glories, past and present, it is the Georgian people who will enchant you most.

The Georgians are rightly celebrated for their welcome to strangers who visit them in peace. Their hospitality is unparalleled. Visitors learn very quickly when they first experience a Georgian 'supra' feast laid out in their honour exactly what Georgians mean when they say: 'A guest is a gift from God.'

So this is a story of happy times in Georgia. It is a story of hard work and play, serious feasting, bizarre happenings, nail-biting journeys, poignant moments and constant fun. It tells how I, an innocent Irish fellow, threatened the life of Georgia's President on my first evening, but finished the evening introducing his bodyguards to the delights of Irish Whiskey. You will hear how I attended a dinner where Jesus was a guest; had a close encounter with Stalin's bed and bathroom; walked on the grave of a twelfth century king at his invitation, then helped to cure a sick cow in the High Caucasus, travelled through the Valley of the Devil to the Gates of the Alans, and how I somehow survived that magnificent Georgian institution, the never-ending supra. But above all, I hope it will introduce you to Georgia's generous friendly people, to its delicious food and wine, its mystical form of Christianity, and to its past triumphs and troubles which help to explain some of its present problems.

The Georgia I knew was still different from the rest of the world, with differences that are intriguing. And where the way of life in Georgia is familiar to us, those similarities call to mind a more easy-going leisurely age now largely lost to us in the West, even in Ireland, once so proud of its more laid-back approach to life.

Chapter 1

'You are threatening the life of our president!'

'What Georgia is that?' asked the woman on the other end of the phone in the Belfast travel agents. 'I've only ever heard of the Georgia in the United States. Are you quite sure there is another one?'

'Oh there is,' I said, 'I've got a job there. It's the Georgia that was part of the old Soviet Union....in the Caucasus... between the Black Sea and the Caspian.'

'My Lord, are you wise!' said the woman. 'It doesn't sound too safe to me! Well, we'll try to get you there, but I'm not too sure about the insurance. We'll have to see! Oh, your Georgia has just come up on my screen,' she said, still with some disbelief. 'It certainly looks…,' there was a pause, '… different!'

She was both right and wrong. From the time I arrived at 4:00 a.m. in the hotel in the Georgian capital, Tbilisi, on a cold January morning, until I left several months later, I was to discover Georgia was indeed magnificently different. But I was to learn also that there are striking similarities to Ireland in terms of history, religion and culture, and above all in the Georgians' determination to have a good time whatever tribulations come their way.

'Rifles must be left at reception'

I hadn't paid much attention to the two guys on the bus that had brought us from Tbilisi airport to our hotel and, in my half awake state, even less when they lined up beside me to check in at the reception desk. They had only registered with me as two Americans – one as short and burly as the other was tall and frail – who seemed to know each other, and who, from snatches I had heard of their conversation, had been to Georgia before. How could I have guessed the impact they were both to have on my time in Georgia, and the experiences we were to have together?

'Well, it's still here!' exclaimed the short, burly one, pointing to a notice on the reception desk. I focused on the notice, written in Georgian, Russian and English, and read with alarm, 'Hand guns can be taken to your room; rifles must be left at reception'.

'Is that a joke?' I asked the Yanks.

'It wasn't when we were last here,' said the thin one, 'then this hotel was a hive of gun-tooters, drug dealers and all sorts of….,' he tailed off to cast a glance round the lobby to see if any of these unsavoury characters were still around and within earshot, '…. but I hear things have changed for the better,' he said raising his voice when he saw the lobby was empty. 'They must have, or the Ministry wouldn't let us stay here.'

'Care to bet!' said his friend looking up from his registration form. 'So Frank, you think the Ministry will have cased this joint just for our benefit! Things must have changed round here if they have gotten that organised.'

I didn't know it at the time, but this little exchange was to be typical of these men's approach to our many and varied adventures in Georgia, one always trying to be optimistic, come what may, and the other always deeply sceptical.

'Say, that accent is a give-away,' said the burly one. 'You from Ireland? My great grandmother came from County Clare. What are you doing here?'

I explained.

'Well isn't that something! Frank here and I are working in the same Ministry on the same project as you. I guess we may be seeing a lot of each other from here on.'

'But the notice,' I said, for I was now thoroughly awake and curiosity, not to say fright, was getting the better of me, 'is this place really bristling with hardware?'

'Used to be … maybe still is,' said the burly one, but I could see this was designed to tease his nervous friend. 'But what need you care coming from Ireland. Haven't you got the most bombed hotels in the world right there in Belfast?'

The man behind the reception desk had been listening attentively to this whole exchange, and now felt he must do what he could to restore the honour of his hotel.

'There are no guns here now,' he said firmly. 'The notice has been left to,' he paused to find an appropriate English word, 'to amuse our guests. I have told management that it should be removed. It is no longer relevant.' He turned away abruptly to find our room keys.

'Pity,' said the burly American. 'Just goes to show that Georgia is getting more like everywhere else by the day. My name is Mitch by the way,' and he offered me his hand, 'and this is Frank. Catch up with you sometime tomorrow. I want to know all about County Clare.' And with that they both disappeared towards the lift.

Dining and Dire Warnings

I didn't see Mitch or Frank next day because we were all catching up with sleep and so eating in the hotel restaurant at odd times. The hotel was beautifully situated on a high cliff overlooking Tbilisi and the river Mtkvari, which runs through the ancient heart of the city. In the restaurant, I had been completely taken aback by both the variety and the strangeness of the food for I was ignorant of the fact that Georgia has its own culinary tradition, that it is like nowhere else on earth, and that it is delicious. I had slept through breakfast and lunch so my first encounter with a Georgian menu was at dinner. It was written in Georgian, Russian and English but there the concession to internationalism ended for the food was exclusively Georgian. The waitress came to my aid, and with her help I embarked on a lemon chicken soup called chikhirtma followed by tevzi which was fish served with pomegranate sauce. There were side dishes of soko which turned out to be mushrooms in cream, and cabbage with walnuts called kombostos.

The waitress also kept filling up a plate with the Georgian

staple called khachapuri, which is a delicious, if fattening, cheese pie. Fresh peaches in yogurt finished me off. I had heard about the fine quality of Georgian wine – a friend back in Ireland had assured me that the Georgians had actually invented wine – and, again, the waitress advised me on what to try. On her recommendation, I chose the velvety, ruby-red Mukuzani. I thought I had asked for a glass but she arrived with an uncorked full bottle and, thinking it would have been churlish to refuse, I set to work on both bottle and food.

Throughout my stay in Georgia, I often found myself on steep learning curves, and so it was with this first encounter with their food and drink. Both are superb in terms of quality and quantity, but even an Irishman needs to pace himself at the Georgian table, and I did not pace myself well that first evening. As I left the restaurant, I was not so much walking as floating towards the lift and so on to my room on the 9th floor.

Feeling in need of a breath of air, I stepped out on to the small veranda that overlooked the city. It was now dark, and out there on the scatter of steep hills on the far side of the river, I could see Tbilisi's many churches with their pepper-pot towers, and also the ancient Persian citadel, all brightly illuminated against the night sky. Perhaps it was partly the wine but they had the appearance of floating in mid air. This magical scene must be captured for the folk back home, I thought, as I fished my camera out of my luggage. I had taken my third or fourth flash photo when my phone rang. It was reception and the voice on the other end was verging on the hysterical!

'Please, please, come back into your room, and stop whatever you are doing,' the voice implored. 'You are threatening the life of our President!'

'What have I done wrong?' I asked, thinking that in my inebriated state I had inadvertently dropped something from my veranda on someone's head far below.

'You are aiming something at our President,' said the voice, now sinking to a whisper.

I thought I was hearing things, "What President? Aiming

what? I asked. 'I was only taking photographs of Tbilisi at night.'

'The Georgian President and his wife are dining at the restaurant down below on the other side of the road, and in the darkness their bodyguards think you were aiming a rifle at them. It must be the flash from your camera that has alarmed them. Please stop immediately. They say they will not warn you again. They will shoot!'

Even life in Northern Ireland for thirty troubled years had not prepared me for the accusation that I was threatening the life of a country's president, but my earlier excess of wine came to my aid and helped me to take it calmly. I closed my veranda door, pulled the curtains, and lay down on my bed to savour the novelty of the occasion. Lying there in the darkness, and still emboldened with the good Georgian wine, I got to thinking that I should not miss the opportunity to get a photograph of the President and Georgia's first lady at ground level so to speak. So I foolishly teetered off in search of my first Georgian scoop!

'Scotch is a Woman's Drink!'

I crossed the busy road from the hotel to the restaurant, and mingled with the group of muscle-bound men clad in black leather greatcoats milling about on the pavement. No one questioned me as I pushed my way through to where an enormous black limousine was parked in the restaurant driveway. It had curtains, was obviously armour-plated, and was bedecked with two colourful pennants. I produced my camera, and then all hell broke loose! I was grabbed by both arms by two of the guards and frog-marched away from the car.

'I only wanted to take a picture of the pennants...that was all!' I managed to stammer.

'Who are you? What are you up to? Who sent you? Where are you from?' the questions came thick and fast. I explained that I was the hotel guest that they had spotted earlier, that I had come to apologise for the alarm I had caused, and that I meant no harm to anyone. Reluctantly, they eased their grip on my arms.

'You can't take close-up pictures of the President's car. It's forbidden, and that's final!' one of the black-clad figures hissed at me.

'OK,' I said, 'I'm sorry.' I then decided to play the Irish card which often serves us well in foreign parts.

'I'm from Ireland,' I said, 'and I've come to work in Georgia. Can I at least stand here and see your President as he leaves the restaurant?'

'So long as you stand behind us and don't take pictures,' said a thin- faced guard, 'and you must hand over your camera until the President has left.' I handed him my camera. 'From Ireland.' he continued with a grin. ' Ireland good! Good whiskey from Ireland. I like 'White Horse' whisky – too much!' and he and his mates laughed.

I couldn't let this pass. 'White Horse is Scotch whisky.... from Scotland, not Ireland.' And I tried to look wounded by their bad mistake. My correction clearly puzzled them, so I took my life in my hands and said, 'Scotch whisky is a woman's drink. Men drink Irish whiskey. It's the real thing!'

This obviously touched a raw nerve.

'Tell us the name of an Irish whiskey?' said thin face.

'Oh there are so many,' I said. 'Have you never drunk Bushmills or Jameson whiskey? They are a real man's drink' I said, sensing my arrows were hitting home! They muttered to each other in Georgian.

'My friend and I want to try this Irish whiskey,' said thin-face. 'Where can we get it?'

'In the hotel bar over there.' I said pointing, knowing the bar served both Bushmills and Jameson.

'When our President leaves, we are off duty. You will take us to the hotel bar, and we will drink your Irish whiskey. We will buy for you too,' he added in case I was in doubt.

'It's a deal,' I said, 'but only if you allow me to take a picture of the President's car.'

Again they muttered together. 'OK,' said thin face, 'but I will take the picture for you.'

Armed with my camera, he started to push his way through his leather-clad comrades towards the presidential car. Just at that moment there was a flurry of activity at the entrance to the restaurant, the rear door of the car was thrown opened on the far side, and a distinguished looking man and beautifully dressed lady were unceremoniously bundled into the limo. The door slammed, and they were off into the night followed by two other cars bristling with bodyguards. Several others were left behind on the pavement including my two friends. The one with my camera came back to where I was standing.

'No photo,' he said bluntly, and then added rather sheepishly... 'Too late!' As if to dismiss any protest I might make about our earlier 'deal' being off, he continued briskly, 'Now we go and drink Irish Whiskey,' in a tone that did not brook any argument.

I hastily decided that the best policy was to honour my side of the bargain and take the opportunity it presented to promote the home product so I led the way across the road. My new found friends were called Kote and Ilia, and we were soon all ensconced in the luxurious hotel lobby helping ourselves to glass after glass of the best of Irish from the litre sized bottle that Kote had bought in the bar. As the night wore on and the bottle emptied, I felt duty bound to ask, 'Well! How do you like our Irish Whiskey?'

'It is not so,' Ilia sought for a word 'gentle as Scotch,' he ventured.

'Yes,' I said, 'That is why women like Scotch – because it is smooth like brandy, but it has not got the same "kick" as this Irish whiskey.' I felt safe enough making these sexist remarks since I was sure political correctness would not weigh too heavily with Kote and Ilia, that is if they had ever heard of it.

'Yes,' said Kote, with the intense conviction of the highly inebriated, 'Irish whiskey is a man's drink. We will tell all our friends,' he added, getting shakily to his feet and heading towards the bar to buy another bottle.

'Trust the Irish!'

What with the wine at dinner and the whiskey later, I was in a fairly delicate state next morning when I finally met up again with Mitch and Frank. It was Sunday, and I came across them drinking coffee in the hotel café. I was badly in need of several strong cups so I joined them, and recounted my experiences of the previous evening.

'Trust the Irish,' said Mitch. 'Trust you to get accused of an assassination attempt before you even start your assignment. And I'm sure you can't even name their President, never mind are planning to shoot him?'

I didn't know his name, but Frank came to my rescue.

'He's called Michael Saakashvili. He is an American-trained lawyer, and I'm thankful to say very pro-American. He had President Bush visit Georgia a while ago, partly to spite the Russians, who are up to every trick in the book here. I'm not saying they were behind it but there is a guy standing trial just now for getting up close to Bush and Saakashavili with a hand grenade during the visit. I suppose that's why they are so concerned about Saakashvili's safety, and why you ran into that trouble last night.'

'But he then went looking for more trouble!' exclaimed Mitch looking at me with a mischievous grin 'Say,' he continued, 'whose team are you serving on in the Ministry? Do you know yet?'

I told them, and so we discovered we had all been assigned to the same team. 'That's great,' said Mitch, 'that team needs a bit of livening up. Doesn't it Frank?'

Frank didn't look too sure so I came to his rescue this time and said, 'The team leader is called Tamuna. What is she like?'

Frank was back on safe ground and replied, 'She's good. Very thoughtful and clever and easy to work with, and so are the other Georgian members of the team. They are mostly women, and they are so nice even when they don't agree with a word we say.'

'Which is most of the time,' Mitch added, and then said thoughtfully. 'I agree. Delightful people. Never worked with nicer. But they are tarred with the same brush as the rest of the officials in Georgia, and in all the other so-called recovering economies of the old Soviet Empire. They will the ends but not the means. You can judge for yourself, but, in my view, Ministry meetings are a bit of a shambles. They don't keep minutes; they don't have an agenda. They abandon the meeting on any pretext. And they will go to any lengths to avoid making a decision. If you push them, they say – 'In Soviet days we were told what to do, we were not asked, so decisions are difficult for us … but we will make a decision…. tomorrow.' But they seldom do! By tomorrow they have drowned themselves in yet more paper from the internet. One day they think the best way of doing something or other is to copy the way it's done in, say, Virginia; the next day its Scotland, then Holland …or Finland and so it goes on. I don't think we've ever heard them say Ireland, have we, Frank?' he paused, and now I was being teased.

'All that is about to change,' I said. 'Why do you think I'm here?' and for a moment they both looked at me seriously. Then we all laughed.

'I think you are being too hard on our Georgian colleagues,' Frank said to Mitch. 'They are doing their best to get in tune with the West's way of doing things, and we can only do what we can to help them. After all, they know best what might work here in Georgia.'

Righteousness and Ram's horns

As the days and weeks went on and I worked closely with these men, I came to respect both for their commitment to indeed doing their best for Georgia. Frank was unfailingly polite, and a man of the highest integrity, but he had a hard time of it for he was a committed evangelical Christian who saw the world, and most of its problems, in black and white terms, and the free and easy way of the Georgians got to him at times. What got to him even more was their love of wine, and their tradition of toasting everyone and everything, living and dead, at their supra banquets, which they organised at every conceivable opportunity, and which went on for hours when Frank wanted to get work done or just get to bed.

'I could get through the supras,' Frank would say, 'if only they would give you the drink in a glass, but they will insist in giving it to you in that darn ram's horn thing which you can't put it down until you have drained it or you spill it on the table, and then they are offended.'

Frank greatly mystified the Georgians by his determined abstinence and, since drinking toasts at supras was inescapable, he would put the horn full of wine to his lips and then quickly pass it to Mitch or to me.

'Oh, so it doesn't matter if we go to Hell,' Mitch would tease him, 'just so long as you stay on the right path!'

Frank stuck to his principles throughout our stay, but there were times when we wished he could have been a bit more flexible, for some of our generous Georgians hosts simply could not comprehend his motives, and clearly took great offence.

Mitch's outlook on life was entirely different. He had mastered that most difficult skill of taking his work very seriously but not taking himself too seriously. He was brilliant at summing up a situation and seeing a way through, and he had a wonderful eye for the ridiculous! In contrast to the idealistic Frank, he was also healthily sceptical of what we could achieve given the different culture and approaches we regularly ran up against and, unusually for an American, he was a master of irony. His impromptu asides were priceless, and he was a much-needed foil to the earnest Frank. Mitch's weakness was that he took strong dislikes to people for no apparently good reason, and certainly did not suffer fools gladly. His less than tactful comments led, on occasions, to damaging tensions with other teams and also with some Georgian officials. Fortunately we three, and indeed the other Georgian members of Tamuna's team, got along very well together, achieved quite a lot in the end, and in the meantime Mitch, Frank and I had the time of our lives.

Chapter 2

Two Christmases in one year

We had arrived in Georgia on their Orthodox Christmas Eve, for the Orthodox Christmas is considerably later than ours, to take up jobs as 'Foreign Experts' in the Ministry, and nobody wanted to see us or to talk about work.

'Did you not know it was their Christmas?' I said accusingly to Frank and Mitch. 'If I'd known, I'd have stayed away until their festivities were over.'

'They were all getting ready to celebrate our Christmas when we left,' Frank explained. 'But I didn't know they have another Christmas of their own! Did you know?' he turned to Mitch.

'Just be thankful if this one doesn't last until Easter,' Mitch retorted. 'God alone knows when they celebrate that, or how long this vacation will last.'

Church is the last place for conversions!

'You have arrived safely,' the woman's soft voice at the other end of the phone woke me, and brought some semblance of normality and reassurance after my bizarre initiation into life in Georgia. 'It is our Orthodox Christmas Eve. Do you want to go to church?'

This wasn't quite how I had envisaged getting acquainted with Tamuna, my new boss, but it was an opportunity to meet informally and, after all, Christmas is Christmas, and the opportunity to celebrate it twice was not to be missed.

'That would be great,' I said. Tamuna then asked me if I had met Mitch and Frank.

'If they want to come too, Lado, our driver, will call for you all at ten this evening; the service starts at eleven.' As it turned out, Lado was to be our official driver for much of our stay, and sometimes doubled as a sort of informal guard in this land where the kidnapping and ransoming of Westerners had, until recently, been something of a national pastime. When I put the prospect of going to church to Mitch and Frank, I could see it put them both in a dilemma, but for quite different reasons. It was clear that Mitch didn't want to go but didn't want to offend Tamuna, whom he clearly held in high regard. Frank liked the idea of 'going to church' but his evangelical form of Christianity made him wary of seeming to approve of other – what he gently referred to as 'mistaken' – forms of Christian worship.

'Oh Hell,' said Mitch, 'let's all go. If we let this Irishman out on his own, God knows what will happen to him next. Last night he tried to shoot their President. Tonight he might try to elope with their Archbishop or whatever they call the boss-man of the Orthodox outfit here. And, Frank, you can give out a few of your 'born again' tracts and maybe win a few converts.'

The ever earnest Frank took this seriously and said thoughtfully, 'They are very touchy about what they call "American religions" here. I could be run out of town. There is a time and a place for conversions, and I doubt if an Orthodox Church service is the place.'

'Well there is the "show-stopping" statement of the week,' said Mitch laughing. 'Anyway, I was only kidding. But let's all go and see what we make of it.'

Long services and short fuses

Lado arrived in the Ministry jeep well after 10 p.m. for I soon discovered that the Georgian attitude to time is delightfully like ours used to be in Ireland before we started taking life so seriously. We found Tamuna and Nana and Eka, two of the other Georgian team members we were to work with in the months ahead, already in the jeep

'We will attend the service in our new Cathedral,' said Tamuna. 'It is very beautiful.'

And so it was. A symbol of Georgia's restored devotion to

their distinct and ancient form of Orthodox Christianity which now goes hand in hand with Georgia's national fervour.

'How long will the service last?' asked Mitch.

'Oh about six or seven hours,' said Nana casually. 'We can't leave before the President which will be around six in the morning.' Frank and I took this on the chin but Mitch was horror struck and, realising he was well and truly trapped, glared at us and said crossly,

'Can you imagine anyone back home – even your crowd Frank – sticking with a church service for six hours? They would all be having withdrawal symptoms from their laptops and cell phones!'

'The spoilt children of the world!'

Getting to the new cathedral in Tbilisi wasn't easy. Some of the streets, and indeed many of the roads throughout Georgia, are in serious need of attention, with potholes verging on the size of craters. The roads up to the cathedral were, at that time, as bad as any we were to encounter anywhere in Georgia throughout our stay.

'This part of our city has been badly hit by earthquakes recently,' said Eka, 'and there is no money to fix the roads at present. They will be fixed when Georgia has attended to other priorities like reforming our army and education.' As she was speaking, Lado seems to be negotiating a near vertical, deeply rutted bank with an alarming drop immediately to our left.

'This is your chance to test the power of prayer,' Mitch whispered to Frank.

Perhaps it was the combination of Frank's prayers and Lado driving but we got to the cathedral eventually. We never ceased to be amazed at what the Georgians put up with, and greet with a smile. Things we take for granted – like well-surfaced roads, streets and pavements – are in many places as yet an aspiration in Georgia. Frank constantly reflected how much we could learn from Georgians' patience, and their determination not to complain about anything.

'Yep,' Mitch would say now and again, 'I wish their optimism was infectious. Their motto seems to be – "Today is good; tomorrow will be better!" – compared with ours in the West – "Today is bad; tomorrow will be worse!"' And I couldn't but reflect that Mitch was from the great US 'can-do' society. What would he make of our passion for pessimism back home!

'We are dreadfully spoiled in the West,' Frank would say when we encountered yet another of Georgia's genuine needs. 'We really are the spoiled children of the world?'

The communists must be rotating in their graves!

'Look at the crowds,' exclaimed Nana, and there were indeed waves of people surging towards the rock platform on which Tbilisi's beautiful new cathedral stands.

'Tbilisi's ancient cathedral stood on this same site,' Nana explained. 'It was blown up in Stalin's time because the official Communist policy was atheism, but we have rebuilt it as good as new,' she said in her matter of fact way.

We joined one fast moving throng, with pushing and heaving that reminded me of an ill-managed rugby scrum. The crucial difference was that everyone in this scrum was carrying a lighted candle with naked flames, and with hot candle grease dripping everywhere. We were jammed up against a narrow gateway to the Cathedral grounds which seemed to be under the control of a group of teenage lads who were determined to allow access only through one side of the gate. Our Georgian friends took hold of our arms knowing that if we got separated from them in this massive crowd, not speaking a word of Georgian in a remote part of a strange city, we could be in real difficulty. Eventually we got through the gateway, and were carried by the crowd to the avenue leading to the cathedral's main entrance, there to await the arrival of Georgia's President and Orthodox Catholicos-Patriarch. The latter arrived first, dressed in magnificent golden robes with matching crown, and accompanied by incense bearers and a choir of young men singing the polyphonic chants unique to Georgia. In the dark of that winter night, with thousands of hand-held candles glowing around the cathedral, looking out over Tbilisi with its other churches also radiant with light, the scene was other-worldly.

When the Catholicos-Patriarch and his entourage had entered the church, it was then President Saakashvili's turn. He and his followers got out of their limos and literally sprinted up the avenue into the church.

'He runs everywhere,' said Nana, 'because he has a lot to do to get Georgia on the path of recovery.'

'Or maybe he is scared of getting shot!' said the more prosaic Eka. 'Yea or maybe he has heard you are here and still gunning for him!' Mitch muttered to me.

It is certainly true that President Mikheil Saakashvili has quite a job on his hands in overseeing Georgia's full and speedy recovery from the devastation wrought by the command economy of Soviet times. Georgia also has its dissidents who would not be averse to pulling a gun or throwing a hand grenade at the President whom some hold accountable for past ills or present difficulties. In the course of our work in Georgia, we met some of the 150 thousand refugees who were forced to flee to the safety of Tbilisi from the breakaway provinces. Most of them had dreadful tales to tell of the loss of relatives, possessions and livelihoods, and very few, understandably, are willing to put the past behind them.

'Now we must somehow get into the cathedral itself!' said Tamuna. Again the crowd surged forward, this time towards the church's great double entrance doors which, like the gates earlier, were manned by a group of boys, and were only half open.

'Is this "half-open door" policy some kind of crazy Georgian tradition or is it just mismanagement?' Frank pondered as the crush to get in grew intolerable.

With the life being squeezed out of us, and with our friends again holding onto us, we were carried bodily into the church. And there we stood for a full six hours – for there are few seats in Orthodox churches – buoyed up with the intoxicating ethereal Orthodox music, and marvelling at a religious fervour which I had never experienced before in any other church anywhere.

In so far as I could gather my thoughts about the scene before me, I pondered that one reason for this intense fervour may be seventy years of enforced atheism by Soviet Russia combined with Georgia's rejuvenated national fervour for both church and state.

When I reflected on all this to Mitch later he said, 'Georgians are very conscious of present day 'enemies' within and without, and they wear their religion like a kind of national 'badge'. They are understandably proud of a form of worship which is uniquely Georgian and which is almost as ancient as the Georgian state itself. You know that, apart from their neighbour Armenia, Georgia was the second country in the world to adopt Christianity as the national religion way back in the fourth century, and they have carried on in their own sweet way ever since.'

'What amazed me most,' said Frank, 'was the mass of young people in the Cathedral, all taking the service so seriously, crossing themselves in that strange Orthodox way, and joining with such fervour in all the ritual and responses. Their former atheist communist leaders must be rotating in their graves!'

And how were we all faring back in the cathedral three, four or five hours into the ceremony? I confess I would have fallen down several times, if only there had been any space, so in best stoical Irish fashion I 'stood my ground' and watched the amazing spectacle. My companions were being equally stoical except for Frank who clearly was becoming increasingly agitated as the ceremony progressed, and was shifting from one foot to the other.

'What's the matter Frank,' I whispered in his ear, 'is all this ritual too much for a good Evangelical?'

'Believe me that is the least of my worries just now,' he stammered, 'I need to get to the bathroom but how can I possibly get out of here?'

I could see his problem. Not only did it seem impossible to get through that throng to a door, but we had been warned by our Georgian colleagues that no one was allowed to leave the church until the President left. I whispered Frank's problem to the ever practical Mitch.

'Tell him to try and not think about it, or to cross his legs or something. That is all I can suggest,' said Mitch, not showing much sympathy, 'and tell him not to mention it again or we will all soon get the urge.'

I didn't feel this was much help, so didn't pass the advice on. I could see that Frank was now trying to resolve this all too human dilemma by keeping his eyes tight shut, contorting his face and clasping his hands in front of him in the manner of fervent prayer.

He soon caught Tamuna's attention. 'It is wonderful to see Frank so deeply moved by our church rituals,' she whispered, 'I thought he might not approve.'

'Something is moving him,' Mitch whispered back, 'but it's not the service.' He continued to whisper to Tamuna who promptly took Frank by the arm and, using her candle like a baton to force a passage through the crowd, spirited him away. When we met them again outside much later, no details of what had subsequently transpired were sought or given. Clearly Mitch and I had come to the same conclusion that 'there but for the grace of God …!'

They shoot your tyres if you don't drink with them!

'This afternoon you must come to our Christmas Day supra,' said Tamuna as Lado drove us back to our hotel in a blizzard which made the journey even more hazardous than the one to get there.

'What is this?' I thought. 'Some kind of meeting in the Ministry, and on Christmas Day! Surely not!'

Again I consulted my American friends and was told that the supra is a unique time-honoured Georgian feast which, like their church services, can last for hours but with the difference that the time is spent in solid eating, drinking, toasting and singing.

'So it's like an Irish party,' I said. 'Well thankfully I've had lots of practice over the years so I don't think their supras holds any terrors for me.'

'Your Irish party will be some help,' Mitch explained grinning, 'and will certainly have got you into the spirit of the Georgian supra, but it's actually a more complicated affair than you think, and still a bit strange for us in the West. Georgian food is stunning, of course, but at the supra it arrives at the table in vast quantities and in such variety! You must eat some of everything or you offend the woman of the house, and you must join in all the toasts or you'll offend the toastmaster – the Tamada – who is usually the host. But you somehow must not get up from the supra table either full drunk or entirely sober! You can try to get this right but really only the Georgians can manage to strike the balance. But hey, don't let our experience put you off. Just go and enjoy yourself, and we'll be interested to hear how an Irishman deals with the supra. If you don't survive it entirely intact, you can take comfort in the fact that the Georgians there have had lots of practice at managing themselves at supras. They organise them at the drop of a hat!'

'There is no escaping them.' Frank added with feeling. 'I don't approve of all that toasting but the visitor is held in great honour in Georgia, and the supra is their way of displaying their respect for the stranger so I have had to cope bearing that in mind. It puts me in a very difficult position because I won't touch alcohol, and the Georgians don't understand that at all. Refusing to drink with them seems to be the only thing that really offends them. I've heard of them shooting up the tyres of visitors' vehicles when folk have refused to join them in a supra, though I think that may have been up in the High Caucasus,'

During my stay, I was to sample many supras from the Black Sea to the Caspian, from high mountain villages in the Northern Caucasus to 'take-out' supras close to Georgia's southern border with Turkey. And it is true, even for us party-loving Irish, the supra can be a bit of a challenge. In the end, though, I can say of this wonderful form of hospitality you have not truly lived until you have sampled the variety of Georgian cooking set before you at a supra, and you have not died and gone to heaven until you have sampled Georgia's wonderful wines.

That said, Georgia is not a country for slimmers or teetotallers!

Welcome to the land of never-ending supras!

So next afternoon it was off to experience the Georgian Christmas supra.

'Why are you two not coming?' I asked suspiciously, when I discovered I was not going to be accompanied by my two friends.

'Frank doesn't feel too good,' said Mitch winking at me knowingly, 'and I've got a pressing invitation to visit our Embassy down town. The Embassy folk obviously only believes in celebrating one Christmas in the year! I'm sorry to miss it, and sorry to abandon you, but you're on your own on this one.'

I must have looked disappointed for he added, 'Like I say, the Irish party scene will mean you're in good training for the supra, I hope!' he added with a mischievous grin, 'and don't worry, there will be plenty more for us all to attend together. You are now in the land of never ending supras!'

Chapter 3

Jesus comes to dinner

'The Irish drink up good like us Georgians.'

Twelfth century Georgian Icon. The Presentation in the Temple

'No, no,' said Tamuna, 'you must learn to drink toasts like a Georgian! Once only to the lips, and then 'down the hatch' as the Americans say. If you sip it like that we will think you Irish drink like old ladies!' Thus warned, and with the reputation of Ireland hanging in the balance, I quickly learned to drink toasts like a Georgian. A bittersweet lesson!

It was the Orthodox Christmas Day and Andreo, a doctor, and his wife, Manana, had invited Frank, Mitch and me to the

Christmas supra in their home. In the end I went on my own feeling oddly apprehensive about attending a family gathering where I scarcely knew anyone, and after all I had already heard about the niceties of supras. I need not have worried. There were enough friends and neighbours of our hosts present to get the supra off to a rousing start, and some students from the University of Tbilisi who had not gone home for Christmas added to the great goodwill and party spirit. I was immediately made to feel very much at home and part of the family. Of all the many supras I was to attend, including a funeral supra, Manana and Andreo's Christmas supra remains the most vivid, for a number of reasons, some good, some bad! I remember arriving at their home, I recall the tables laden with delicious food, I recall being bewildered by all the toasts, I recall the singing (and even contributing with – I think – a rendering of 'Danny Boy') but I have no recollection of how things ended, of getting back to my hotel or of anything else for a full day later. I took some comfort from Lado's comment that, 'You Irish can drink up good like us Georgians. Like us, you enjoy a good supra'. Lado must have got me safely back to the hotel that Orthodox Christmas night and for that I will always be grateful. I was to learn over the coming months that Lado was a great supra-goer himself, and on occasions did not pace himself too well either. From time to time Tamuna would call us in the morning saying, 'Lado is unwell this morning. I am sending a taxi for you'. That brought memories of the Christmas supra flooding back to me, and I would think of Lado with a mixture of envy and sympathy. At all succeeding supras, I had to learn that most difficult of lessons in Georgia – the art of moderation in the face of excess.

God's gift to Georgians

The Supra is not just a meal, it is how the exuberant Georgian nation regularly celebrates simply being Georgian and just how proud they are of that. Feasting in this way is a very ancient tradition and is testimony to the fact that Georgia, with such a rich soil and wonderful climate, is a land of plenty. It not only produces all the farm produce with which we in Ireland are familiar but also its own tea on the shores of the Black Sea and, of course, its magnificent wines just about everywhere but especially in the lands near the Caspian.

When I mentioned to Tamuna once that Ireland and Georgia had much in common, she laughed and said, 'I would like to visit Ireland for I have always heard it is a beautiful country but we Georgians know in our hearts that there is nowhere in the world like Georgia. We have a story that when God was giving out land to all the peoples of the earth we Georgians were attending a supra, and we arrived late before the Almighty's throne. God explained that all the land had been given away, and was angry with us. But when our ancestors explained that they had been feasting at a supra, and raising their glasses in praise of the Almighty, God was so pleased that he gave the Georgians the part of the earth he had been keeping for himself. So that is how we Georgians came to inhabit the most beautiful country in the world.'

Coming to Terms with Supras and Armenians

Back at Manana and Andreo's home, the Christmas supra was in full swing, and was more than proving its worth as a demonstration of Georgian generosity, hospitality to the stranger, and as a bonding session for the Georgians present. They lost no time affirming their solidarity, and sharing their current concerns about, and yearning for, national unity. I noticed that Eka, one of my Ministry colleagues, was not joining in the toasts, and I asked her why.

'I will not drink,' she said darkly, 'until all the Russians have left my country and Georgia is united again.' This reference to Russia's continued influence in Georgia, and the pressure it exerts on the country, is a national pre-occupation. The Russians are furious with the Georgians for cosying up to the Americans and to the West, and are showing their displeasure by encouraging some of the Georgian provinces to break away. At its most dramatic, this 'encouragement' has recently taken the form of an actual Russian invasion of part of Georgia. During our stay, the pressure was more subtle. The Russians would, from time to time, cut off the electricity and gas supply to Tbilisi or they would refuse to allow the import to the Russian Federation of Georgian wine and mineral water, products Russians themselves have enjoyed for centuries. They already have managed to dislodge the Province of Abkhazia, with its beautiful Black Sea coastline, from Georgian control, and this has led to thousands of refugees flooding into Tbilisi. Most were being housed somehow during our time there, but on any night in the capital, refugees, including many children, could be seen roaming the streets begging, and sleeping rough in bus shelters and other public places. I noticed that people in Tbilisi seldom passed a beggar in the street without making some contribution however small. This was because so many of the beggars were refugees from Abkhazia who have lost everything. South Ossetia, which has a minority Russian population, is a Georgian province where the Russians can also spread discontent, encourage separation, and have most recently invaded. Even during our stay in more settled times, Tamuna would never allow Frank, Mitch or me to accompany the rest of the team there since she said it would not be 'comfortable' for us.

'We are surrounded by enemies,' Eka continued, her sad expression such a contrast to the Christmas festivities going on around her, 'but I am certain we will win in the end because we are Georgians.'

'Are your neighbours to the south, the Armenians, not good friends and supporters,' I asked trying to brighten the conversation and mindful that Armenia, like Georgia, is a small Orthodox Christian country.

'The Armenians!' Eka looked at me as if I was mad, 'No, No, the Armenians are …,' she seemed lost for words.

'Unpredictable friends.' I suggested, now sorry I had opened my mouth.

'No!' she said emphatically, 'they are entirely predictable. They can always be depended on to betray Georgia!'

I knew when I was out of my depth, and went back to eating, toasting and celebrating my second Christmas.

The toasts are a very serious matter at the Georgian supra. Even at the most informal or improvised of supras there is always a Toast Master called a Tamada. He (and, unless there are no men present, the Tamada is always a 'He') rules over the supra benignly but firmly. He regulates the order of the toasts, and calls on others in turn to propose their toast. Andreo, as head of our host family that Christmas afternoon, was the Tamada, and so proposed the first toast. With glasses and rams' horns raised to the ceiling, we were exhorted to acknowledge God Almighty's presence at our table.

'And now,' said Andreo, 'since it is Christmas we must welcome Christ Himself to join our supra.'

The Arrival of Jesus

I thought I was hearing things. But no! At that moment Christ did indeed join us in a manner of speaking. Andreo rose from the table, took a beautiful silver bowl from a shelf, and filled it full of rich red wine from a rather bashed looking plastic bottle

Twelfth century Georgian Icon –
The Appearance of the Holy Spirit

'Father Georgi, our parish priest, gave me this wine at church this morning,' he explained for my benefit. 'It is consecrated so it is the Blood of Christ.' He then proceeded to unwrap a round loaf of bread from a linen cloth, 'And here is His Body too,' he continued. Breaking the bread into several pieces, he placed them and the silver bowl containing the wine on a tray, and began circulating it around the supra table.

'What do I do when it gets to me?' I whispered to Tamuna in some consternation.

'You dip the bread in the wine and eat it,' she said simply. 'It is very special.'

'But I'm not Orthodox ...,' I broke off for I realised that this was not the time to be parading my personal doubts and ill-thought-out theology. To refuse this greatest of gifts from my hosts would give profound offence, so I swallowed my scepticism with the bread and wine and passed the tray on to Eka. I noticed that, despite her vow of abstinence, Eka took the bread and wine.

'Did you not want to take Christ's body and blood because you had not been fasting?' Eka asked me as she passed the tray on. 'It is acceptable to do so,' she continued. 'I once said to my priest that I could not take communion because I had not been fasting, but he said 'God looks into your heart, my child, not your stomach' I then said, 'But Father I know I am not worthy to receive the Saviour.' My priest said. 'And neither am I, my child, or any of us, so receive God's grace and be happy.'

Eka had said all this to reassure me that I had done nothing wrong in taking the bread and wine, and that this was the Georgian way of welcoming Christ into their homes. How could I explain to her that 'unworthiness' was not the baggage I had brought to Andreo and Manana's Christmas supra but something much less well considered – western woolly scepticism.

To move the conversation away from me and my theological problems, I said 'In Western churches, communion is administered by a priest and normally taken in church, and Christian friends of mine, especially Catholic friends, would find it very strange to have the consecrated bread and wine passed round the dinner table at home.'

'Oh your friends must have very modern ideas!' said Nana who had been listening. 'Our Orthodox ways go back right to the Apostles who did it our way, so who can argue with that? Of course only a priest can turn the bread and wine into the Body and Blood of Christ but, after that, it belongs to us all, and is a beautiful way to have Christ come to visit our homes, don't you think?'

'Since the Orthodox form of worship is so ancient,' said I, 'what does the Georgian Orthodox Church think of other Christian religions?'

'The Orthodox do not judge any other religions,' said Nana firmly. 'It would be wrong to do so and can only lead to bad feeling.' Well, if that's the case, I thought, I can't see Orthodoxy making much headway back where I come from, but I said nothing!

'Of course,' said Eka, 'you must not take our word for all this. We were brought up as atheists in Communist times so we are still learning about our Orthodox religion. Would you like to talk to my priest? He will be able to answer all your questions.'

With Christ now firmly in our midst, the Georgians settled down to enjoy His presence and to make merry. The toasts continued – to Manana and the women who had prepared the supra, to all our parents, alive and dead, to our children, to our Mother Lands, to Churchill and Margaret Thatcher, to Georgian culture especially their great twelfth century poet Shota Rustaveli, to Shakespeare (who they could all quote), to Dickens (who they had all read), to Oscar Wilde, to W. B. Yeats, to James Joyce, to Tolstoy. Their knowledge of literature, their own and other peoples' amazed me! Clearly mention of Leo Tolstoy reminded Andreo of something, and he now proposed another toast.

Toasting your Enemies

'To the Russian Government,' he said, 'Raise your glasses!' I was puzzled, but I raised my glass anyway.

'Not the wine glass,' whispered Eka. 'Your beer glass. We Georgians toast our friends in wine but our enemies in beer. Don't misunderstand, we like the Russian people and we love Russian literature and music. We were brought up on it and Russian is our second language. It is the Russian government we don't like.'

I was toasted repeatedly, for Georgians believe that failure to honour a guest in this way amounts to a sin. When it was Andreo's turn to toast me, he quoted from their great poet Rostaveli:

'Spending on feasting and wine is better than hoarding our substance. That which we give makes us richer, that which is hoarded is lost. A guest is a gift from God.'

I felt honoured and humbled at one and the same time.

As the toasting progressed, I noticed that each toast seemed designed to provide all the men present with an opportunity to air an opinion and occasionally a grievance, usually political. The women present took no part in proposing the toasts, and spent most of their time ferrying food and drink to and from the table. Reflecting on this (for to the Western eye it is now not pc) it wasn't so much that the women are kept in their place but that they give their place to the men folk whose duty it then is to honour them for it . Even the highly educated women at Andreo and Manana supra showed no resentment at all at the men hogging the limelight; indeed it did not seem to cross their minds. When I started to pile up some of the plates to make room for even more, Manana (herself a university lecturer) said 'No no, no – that is women's work!'

Tradition demands that you drain your glass at each toast, and often, as Frank had warned me, it isn't even a glass but a ram's horn overflowing with wine which, given its shape, you literally can't put down until it is drained! As the horn passes round the table one guest says to the next, 'May you be emptied of enemies as this horn has been emptied of wine'. The horn is then immediately refilled by the 'Merikipe', the family member or friend whose job it is to make sure the horn and glasses are filled at all times. What saves the day, to some extent, is the array of food the hostess provides in a chaos of plates, bowls and casseroles. Georgians are poor by our standards but no expense is spared when it comes to food and wine, and if ever a table could be said to be laden it is the Georgian supra table.

Edible Poetry

I remarked on this to Nana, who was obviously pleased by the comment. She said, 'The Russian poet, Pushkin, once remarked that "every Georgian dish is a poem", and visitors often say that even the Georgian names of our dishes sound like edible poetry.'

Limited as my experience was so far, I could only agree. A delicious cheese pie called Khachapuri is the staple, as is an unusual spicy meat dish encased in what looks like a purse made from pastry and called khinkali. To savour these 'purses' you nibble a hole in the corner, hold the purse up in the air and let the contents dribble into your mouth. Not elegant but exquisite! Each family has its own unique versions of khachapuri and khinkali and, while they all taste a little different, they are unfailingly delicious.

'How do you like our Georgian khachapuri?' Nana asked me. 'Do you not think it is much better than Italian pizza?'

'Much better' I said, and meant it.

'If only we Georgians had got to the USA in the same numbers as the Italians, it would have been our Khachapuri that would have taken the world by storm and not their pizzas!' Nana sighed. 'For far too long we have been locked into Russia and the other Soviet Republics when we should have been trying to look to the West. Did you know, for example, that almost all the good quality restaurants in Moscow are still Georgian? We have a lot of ground to make up in introducing the West to the wonders of Georgian cooking and our superb Georgian wines. Visitors like you must tell the world about our khachapuri, khinkali and our other unique Georgian dishes.'

'Oh I will,' I assured her. And to honour this undertaking to Nana that Christmas evening, to acknowledge the generosity of the many Georgia hosts during my stay, but, above all, to celebrate and bring to light the best-kept secret that is Georgia's exquisite cuisine, I include a final chapter to do just that so that the whole world can prepare and enjoy a Georgian 'supra'! During the evening the dishes arrive in no particular order, and when plates are empty they are simply removed from the table to make way for still more delicacies. Mindful of Nana's comment about the very names being edible poetry, I asked her and Eka to tell me what each dish was, and what it was called in Georgian. They took it in turns to do so as the plethora of dishes arrived, and that Christmas Day we had lamb with potatoes, aubergine and tomatoes (chanakhi), turkey in walnut sauce (sastsivi), asparagus soup (satatsuri), Georgian egg salad (azelila), beets in cherry sauce (charkhlis chogi), spinach with yogurt (ispanakhi matsvnit), beef stew with pickles (solyanka), kidney beans in plum sauce (lobio tkemali), liver with pomegranate sauce (ghvidzli), a chicken dish called bazhe.... and I think it was at that stage of the toasting my concentration deserted me, and I abandoned my culinary researches! I can vouch for the fact that the very names entice you to sample and then eat more than is good for you. In addition to all this, there were various other sauces, pickles and preserves. And then came the sweets! Candied walnuts (gozinaki), peaches in syrup (atami), lemon and honey cakes and a hazelnut confection rich in calories called churchkhela. Turkish coffee and Georgian tea arrived too late to save me! We had been dining and toasting and singing for a full four hours when I passed out, and I can recall no more.

'You did not disgrace yourself,' Tamuna's voice was, as ever, reassuring at the other end of the phone when I finally woke up next day back in my hotel. 'It was Andreo's job, as our Tamada, not to allow such a thing. No, but you were just exhausted by our Christmas supra. Our visitors often find their first supra a little ... challenging. Anyway,' she continued, 'your enjoyment of our food and wine made Christmas so happy for all of us. You have impressed all the men. They said the Irish must love life as much as we Georgians, and the women who were there now want to meet more Irish men!'

'What did you do to deserve that?' laughed Mitch when I told him. 'I hope I never find out!' I replied.

'We will have our first meeting in the Ministry tomorrow morning,' trilled Tamuna at the end of her call. And that's another story!

Chapter 4

Questioning Karl Marx

Karl Marx's grave, London

'Soso and Peppered Vodka'

'Welcome to the Ministry,' cried Tamuna handing us all a tumbler of peppered vodka from somewhere behind her desk. It was 10:30 on our first morning, and we were making an early start. The Ministry was housed in a strange, highly ornamented building which looked as if it had sprouted from the earth like a sort of exotic artichoke. We were to find nothing exotic inside. Apart from the entrance hall, which had a certain elegance and was, for some reason, always thronged with agitated elderly people, the rest of the interior was a warren of dusty offices distinguished only by the massive height of the ceilings. Long bleak corridors linked the offices, and at the end of each corridor was a toilet which, despite the best efforts of the cleaning staff, was a bit primitive and so best avoided.

'If you want to use the toilet,' Tamuna explained, 'You must use Soso's. I will get you a key.'

I had signed a contract on the internet with someone called 'Soso' and had undertaken to report to him on a regular basis during my stay. It now struck me as amusing that my first real-life encounter with him would be the honour of using his loo. As it turned out, that was the closest, so to speak, I ever got to him. Over the months that I worked in the Ministry, Soso, though always a 'presence', never actually materialised in the flesh. However, that did not stop Tamuna regularly calling on him for assistance, and Mitch, Frank and I soon came to recognise a little ritual involving Soso to which Tamuna resorted from time to time. When, at a meeting, we suggested a way of doing something to which she was reasonably well disposed, Tamuna would say, 'I think that will work well in Georgia – you must write another paper on that.' When we suggested something that seemed feasible but difficult or expensive to implement, she would say, 'I think that might work in Georgia – but not yet'. When she was totally opposed to some suggestion, instead of saying, 'no – never!' she would say, 'I will ask Soso.' She would then disappear into Soso's office and emerge ten or fifteen minutes later saying, 'Soso does not think that will work here.' After a while, the unworthy thought crossed our minds that there was no one actually behind that desk in 'Soso's' office. Could it be, we speculated, that Tamuna went in, closed the door, had a well-deserved rest and a cigarette, and then emerged armed with what we came to call 'a Soso decision' which was, in fact, her's alone? We will never know, for even when we were leaving and suggested, mischievously by that stage, that we should deliver our final report to Soso in person, we were told he was working with the Minister and so too busy to see us. In fact though, whether he existed or not, we came to admire more and more the whole concept of 'Soso' and his 'decisions', and concluded that we would all benefit from a 'Soso' in our lives.

Tamuna's other delightful ploy was her use of peppered vodka. If Mitch, Frank and I were forging ahead too fast or taking Tamuna and the Georgian members of the team too much for granted, she would produce peppered vodka and chocolates from her cupboard saying, 'Let us all relax now and take a break. This will settle our stomachs – and heads.' Apart for poor Frank, whose conscience wouldn't let him touch a drop and who, if he could escape on these occasions, went and hid in Soso's loo, the rest of us simply surrendered to this wonderful Georgian recipe for creative delay which was their way of making progress of a kind.

Meetings Georgian style

All our meeting were held in Tamuna's office, and both the office and the meetings were, as Mitch had predicted when I first arrived, the most delightful shambles. Frank and Mitch, both earnest Ivy League men keen to put the Georgian Ministry on the right – or at any rate the American – track found the lack of such commonplace conventions as an agenda and minutes hard to take. True, we were all on a steep learning curve about each other's approaches and cultures but with the added problem that we were not all on the same curve. On the one hand, the Georgians are keen to prepare their country to join the West, the European Union and indeed NATO at the earliest possible moment, hence the frenetic reform programmes and the employment of all of us Western 'experts' to teach them Western ways. On the other hand, Georgia's unique civilisation, nurtured at this crossroads between Europe and Asia, and with its distinctive language, its rich literature, its long adherence to Orthodox Christianity, its ancient traditions, and, above all, the survival of all of this in the face of innumerable invasions, takeovers, aggressive ideologies and just plain barbarism, makes Georgians wary of adopting the latest bunch of trendy ideas from the West.

'We must be careful how we manage things,' Tamuna would warn us gently, 'when we go out to the regions to consult with the people there about these new ways of doing things. Some may say that we Georgians were a civilized and cultured nation two thousand years ago when people in the West were still swinging about in bushes.'

But it wasn't always differences over how to address the great issues but more often the little things that used to get to the two Americans.

'Wouldn't you think,' said Frank as we made our way home one day after another apparently fruitless round of meetings, 'that they would at least take a note of what we all think we have agreed, cut down on making tea and coffee and passing round all those cookies and chocolates to give us a chance to make some progress. And what about all the interruptions!'

The interruptions to meetings did indeed frustrate all of us. Georgians have taken to the mobile phone with a vengeance, and they never switch it off. They call each other incessantly, and in the middle of explaining some tricky western way of doing things, a Georgian colleague's mobile would ring, and the lengthy call that ensued would invariably disrupt everyone's train of thought, and quite often derail the meeting altogether. I've even known a mobile to ring while a Georgian colleague was delivering a lecture out in the provinces, and she stopped in mid-sentence to take the call.

But mobiles weren't the only distraction to beset our meetings. Anyone from anywhere – be it from up-country, or old Georgian friends back on holiday from the US, the UK or wherever – all felt duty bound to call in Tamuna's office, and everything stopped so that they would be properly greeted, introduced and made welcome. On one occasion, just when Mitch was in full flow explaining something, the door of the office swung open and a woman appeared with a tiny baby. Again everything stopped so that the baby could be admired, cuddled, cradled, passed around, cooed over, and its Georgian names explained in great detail.

'Well at least they didn't bloody well change its nappy,' Mitch muttered through clenched teeth. Frustrating yes! But Georgians mean no disrespect by any of this; it is simply that family, friends and people generally still come first in Georgia. Government Ministers are determined, however, to move Georgia on, and Ministers are the same the world over – full of bright shiny ideas! One morning Tamuna rushed into the office fresh from a meeting with her Minister and announced 'The Minister has come back from Brussels with two new ideas – all institutions under his control are to be provided with state-of-the-art computers and (horror of horrors!) there is to be no more smoking in the Ministry!' The first of these directives could safely be ignored since some of the institutions in question couldn't afford to repair their broken doors and windows never mind provide fancy computers. But the latter! An end to smoking in the Ministry! ... consternation! ... for Tamuna and her Georgian colleagues all smoked like furnaces! A Georgian solution was soon forthcoming to getting around the 'no smoking' directive. For now, in the middle of a meeting, if a Georgian colleague felt the need for a restoring cigarette, she hung out of Tamuna's windows puffing furiously while, yet again, the meeting struggled on as best it could. I've known two of them hanging out the windows at the same time. Poor Mitch and Frank, whose whole approach to life and work could best be summed up as tight, tidy and tireless, were not amused!

'Is it the Queen or the Pope?'

'Discussion and consultation can be a problem for us,' Nana explained one morning. 'In Communist times we were just told what to do. There was no consultation so agendas and minutes were unnecessary. There could be no disagreement and so little to discuss. However, we are now learning to consult, and tomorrow we have organised a consultation in the city of Signaghi about three hours from Tbilisi near the border of Azerbaijan. And we will be able to buy good local wine on the way back for we will travel through the heart of our best wine-growing region', she added with the air of one who was well practiced in multitasking and ferreting out the best wines in the wine-rich Kakheti region.

The next morning Tamuna lent out of her office window

and shouted down to Lado, who was loitering in the Ministry yard smoking with his driver mates, to get ready to take us to Sighnaghi. 'Getting ready' to travel in Georgia wasn't all that easy since many of the country roads are severely potholed so the appropriate kind of car has first to be located in the car pool, and then the best route carefully considered. After much discussion it was finally resolved what route Lado would take, and it proved to be entirely to Nana's satisfaction.

'Good,' she whispered when we were told the travel plans. 'We have a big car on a good road; that means we can bring back more wine, and get it home safely.' Women the world over are wonderful at getting their priorities right!

As we approached Sighnaghi, we remarked on the ancient city walls which seemed to be still largely intact. Eka explained that the city had, for much of its history, been a frontier town famous for its fierce warriors and its independent spirit. From our experience that afternoon, the good citizens were quite determined to live up to this reputation, and the consultation meeting, which was held in a school, verged on the warlike.

'Do not be offended,' Tamuna had warned us once again before the meeting began, 'but we are only here to ask the people's opinion on these issues, not to hear their reaction to your views on how we Georgians should do things.'

'So why the hell did they ask us to write all those papers?' Mitch muttered darkly to me. 'And I'm sure they won't take a note on what is said at this meeting either!'

But they did! The school had produced a primitive type of flip-chart, and on this the comments of the audience were faithfully noted in so far as anyone could hear them, for they all tended to shout at once.

'Maybe we have succeeded in contributing to their culture even if it is only the introduction of the flip-chart,' muttered Mitch dryly as Tamuna and her colleagues struggled to make sense of what was being said.

The first audience comprised a cross section of earnest citizens of the town all determined to make themselves heard above the din. However, this unstructured session was quite orderly compared with the discussions held later with some of the older school pupils. They too were very determined to have their say and shape the future of their country, and they also thought that this could best be achieved by all shouting at once. Somehow a semblance of order was achieved and some coherence put on the welter of comments and suggestions made by the various groups. When the consultation was over, the group of teenage students gathered round me since they had heard I was from Ireland and inevitably they had heard something about our 'Troubles'.

'Ireland is a divided country, right? Is that what the problem is really about?' asked one of them.

While I was thinking where to start, and how to keep the explanation simple, another said, 'Is it not that the Protestants want to be ruled by the Queen and the Catholics by the Pope?' He paused, looked at me, and thinking he had got it wrong added '… or is it the other way round?'

'Well,' I said, 'it is about two groups of people who are unhappy about sharing the country they live in.' This was greeted with blank looks so I continued, 'It is a bit like Georgia's provinces of Abkhazia and South Ossetia.' But now I had clearly touched a very raw nerve!

'Oh that is quite different,' they shouted. 'These regions are Georgian! They belong to us Georgians. It is only the Russians that are encouraging them to break away!'

Why is it, I wondered, that other people's problems always seem so much more manageable than your own?

'Know you David Beckham?'

As I was leaving, and Nana was hurrying us along so that she would have time to shop for that wine on the way back, a teacher of English collared me to go and speak to her English class.

'This man speaks English,' she explained to her class. 'Come along; ask him some questions in English.' There was silence. 'Giorgi, you are not usually shy. Ask the gentleman a question.'

Poor Giorgi turned bright pink and slowly raised his hand,

'Know you David Beckham?' he asked nervously.

Chasing good grapes

On the way back, we called at a number of farms where Nana sampled the wine and then bargained in a very 'gloves-off' robust fashion. All this sampling and bargaining took place in the yard of the farms. The 'yard' is itself something of an institution in Georgia. Except in the big cities, almost everyone has one, and neighbours and passing strangers call in the yard to chat and eat and drink there, for Georgian wine is matured in great underground, often very ancient, vats called kvevri sunk deep in the yard. The kvevri is a veritable wine well, the wooden lid of which is removed to drop tin cups on strings so that you can treat your friends or offer samples. When Nana had got the quality of wine she wanted at the right price, we all stocked up and set off back to Tbilisi.

'With all that sampling.' said Nana. 'I fear I have broken my Easter fast.' Serious fasting before the great Orthodox Church services has come back into its own across Georgia. Many of our colleagues were fasting for Easter, and to my amazement there were even 'fasting menus' in many of the restaurants in Tbilisi.

As we travelled back through the rich agricultural country side, we asked our Georgian friends about farmers like those we had just met, and how they had fared under the Communist collectivation of agriculture when all farm land had been seized and 'pooled'.

'Well,' said Eka, 'The richer farmers around here – they were called Kulaks in Russian; have you heard of them? – well, most were liquidated in Stalin's time, though perhaps the terror may not have been so great in Georgia as elsewhere in other Soviet Republics. Now farmers like those we have just visited are buying the land back when they can afford it.'

'Yes,' said Nana, 'my family were farmers and most of them were murdered by Stalin, and their land seized for the collective farm. They were not even rich, but just wanted to hold on to their own land. My mother only escaped because she was living with my aunt in the city when the rest of the family was rounded up.' She said all this in a matter of fact way, and with no bitterness.

'Are all of you not still very angry at the suffering Communism inflicted on your country?' Mitch demanded with feeling.

'But it was not all bad!' Eka exclaimed. 'In the early days when Communism was being imposed, terrible things were done, but for the next generation – our generation – things were good for a time. For example, we had free education from infant school to university, and our health services were also completely free unlike yours in America.' She paused then continued thoughtfully, 'Still, we would not want the old system back; whatever good things we have lost, and despite some present difficulties, we greatly value our personal freedom which we did not have in Soviet times.'

As we surveyed the beautiful countryside still devastated by poverty and recent oppression, Mitch muttered to me 'When you look at the suffering it has caused, I still think it would have been better if Karl Marx had never bothered writing those bloody books!'

'But has anything Marx said in "Das Kapital" and "The Communist Manifesto" ever really been put into practice in the way Marx envisaged it?' I ventured, clumsily attempting to be provocative. 'Is Communism not a bit like Christianity? It has never really been tried properly.'

'Tell that to Frank,' said Mitch, 'he will be delighted to hear that you think he's a religious fraud.'

But luckily Frank had nodded off in the front seat.

'Tomorrow,' said Tamuna brightly as we were dropped back at the hotel, 'Lado will call for you at 10. We will meet early to collate and make sense of all we have heard today.'

'This I gotta see!' muttered Mitch.

Chapter 5

In the Land of the Svans

Svaneti's famous towers

The interruptions to our meeting in the Ministry were worse than ever that day. Tamuna has several long conversations on the phone while Mitch struggled to keep the meeting going. Then the tea lady arrived and spilt tea over his computer, some guy came to fix Tamuna's printer which resulted in another major upheaval, and finally one of those awkward civil servants that crop up everywhere arrived to have something explained to her, but seemed quite determined not to understand the explanation.

Mitch mopped himself and his computer and said, 'Tamuna! I suppose you haven't got a sign you could hang on the door saying "Do not disturb"'.

As Tamuna pondered what he meant, for the concept seemed

new to her, the office door flew open again.

'Oh holy cow,' growled Mitch as the latest visitor entered. To compound his frustration, in the middle of this visitor's casual chat in Georgian with Tamuna (for that's all it appeared to be) the visitor's mobile rang, and she then broke off for a good five minutes to have a conversation on the phone. By this stage Mitch was attacking his moist computer with yet another tissue, and I had to study my notes to keep from laughing.

'I think it's time for lunch,' said Tamuna brightly when the latest visitor finally left after the usual round of hugs and kisses, thus forestalling a possible irrevocable breakdown in US/Georgian relations. 'But before we go,' she continued, producing a map of Georgia from the compost heap of papers on her desk, 'I must tell you about our next consultation session. It is in Svaneti,' and she pointed to a remote area on the map high up in the northern Caucasus, 'the land of the Svans. This region is the very soul of Georgia. I know you will love it, and the people there,' she added with a dreamy expression.

'I've heard of these Svans,' said Frank as we broke for lunch. 'Until the Tbilisi government sorted them out recently, they were the worst kidnappers of the lot!'

'Oh great!' said Mitch, 'I can see our obituaries now! – '.... and they were never seen again' – I hope your folk back home can find the ransom money,' he said to me. 'I doubt if mine will bother! Of course,' he added, 'it might actually be quiet up there. We might actually get some work done!'

Clearly the many disruptions of the morning had taken their toll!

'Is he 104 or 108?'

'This is Marlen,' said Tamuna as we fell out of a four wheel jeep after the journey of a lifetime, 'he is 104 years old.' I gazed at Marlen in wonder. Tamuna seemed to be checking something with him. 'I'm sorry! Marlen says I'm wrong. He thinks he is 108!'

We had arrived in the land of the Svans – Svaneti – and in my state of mind at that moment, I was prepared to believe anything.

We had just driven at top speed through high mountain passes with vertical sides to our right, sheer drops of unfathomable depth to our left, on a road – I use the term loosely – littered with clay and boulders which our driver Lado took only the most casual steps to avoid, and I was trembling with naked fear.

'Like hell he is,' muttered Mitch, 'we all know the guys faked their age in these parts to avoid being drafted into the Soviet Army.'

'But I thought,' I said, still trying to stop my legs from shaking, 'that they do live forever up here in the High Caucasus. Isn't it because they eat some kind of special yogurt, strange apricots, and have lungs like lions because they breathe this mountain air all their lives.' I had read that somewhere, and I was trying to show Mitch and Frank how relaxed the Irish can be even when faced with instant death at every turn of a steering wheel. 'And haven't they even a famous choir, and you have to be over 100 to get into it?'

Mitch said something unrepeatable implying that the journey and the altitude had clearly affected my head. But I took quiet comfort from the fact that both my American colleagues' faces were as ashen as my own, and that the journey up to Svaneti had scared the wits out of them too. But not Tamuna who looked as calm and composed as ever. It may have been this composure that prompted Frank to say,

'Well, Tamuna we're here. How are we ever to get back down again?'

'It helps if you close your eyes,' she said calmly.

'I thought,' said Mitch, 'that there were times when Lado had closed his! Why did you bring us here, Tamuna? What earthly interest will the good mountain folk up here have in our work?'

'The Svans are part of Georgia!' said Tamuna indignantly. 'In fact,' she said, 'as I told you yesterday, Svaneti is Georgia's beating heart! It is in these high mountains that our ancestors took refuge from our many invaders. It is to these high mountains that we brought all our treasures – our ancient gold and silver objects, our most precious icons, our illustrated manuscripts.

Is it any wonder these have been called "The Mountains of Poetry"?'

'This place has gone to her head too,' muttered Mitch. 'I think I'm now the only sane one around!'

Marlen led the way through the streets of the town, which had several buildings that reminded me of Irish Round Towers except these were all square.

'These ancient towers were our places of refuge in times of danger,' said Tamuna. 'We will hold our meeting in one of them.'

'Surely the changes we are suggesting aren't so dangerous that we have to address the Svans from way up in the air,' said Frank glancing heavenwards.

Tamuna ignored this, and said 'Marlen will translate for us'.

Mitch and I were about to ask the same obvious question when Tamuna beat us to it with an answer. 'Although the Svans are our beating heart,' she said, for she was obviously in poetic mode, 'most do not speak Georgian, or I should say they speak an ancient form of the language like ...' she thought for a moment, 'like your Anglo Saxon.'

'But how will Marlen make sense of all our modern jargon?' asked Frank who had a healthy aversion to acronyms and jargon, was constantly warning us against using them but so far had failed to iron them out of our papers and discussions. All his fears were now coming home to roost in the land of the Svans.

'I will carefully explain them to him,' said Tamuna simply.

Clearly she was not going to allow our negative comments ruin her enjoyment of Georgia's 'beating heart'.

The Svans' Night Out

Whatever language the meeting was conducted in was, as it turned out, largely irrelevant for few were listening. The Svans mustn't get out much, what with their deep valleys and high mountains and being snowed in for eight months of the year, so when they do emerge they obviously like to make a night of it, and it's not to be wasted listening to some blow-ins from way down in Tbilisi talking about changes that they know may never happen, least of all to them. So there we all were, having braved a road that would make the craters of the moon look like child's play, talking in English and American to Tamuna who translated it into Georgian for Marlen who translated it – whatever 'it' was by that stage – into Svaneti, to folk most of whom weren't paying a blind bit of notice. Those who actually sat throughout the meeting often had their back to us, but most wandered about chatting, some seemed to be doing deals, and would slap each other's hands violently when the deal appeared clinched. There seemed to be a plentiful supply of bashed- up plastic bottles which, we learned from Marlen, contained the local hooch and which was fast disappearing as it passed from hand to hand. Most of the audience chain smoked throughout the meeting and, taken all-in-all, this obviously made for a good night out, Svaneti-style! The women were even more intriguing than the men. Many were knitting while catching up with the gossip from their mountain fastnesses, the remoteness of which we could only imagine.

Through the fog of cigarette smoke, we toiled all afternoon. Whatever language the Svans speak, it seems to require you to say 'Caw, Caw', 'Ara, Ara' and 'Rak-hi' a lot. There also seemed to be a sort of unofficial dress code among them, and black leather was definitely in this season. So what with all the Caw Caw-ing and Ara Ara-ing drowning out our efforts at the front (in so far as there was a front), the black leather attire, and the flitting about from bench to bench to clinch deals or not miss out on any gossip, I got to thinking that it all reminded me of something. But what? As usual, Mitch came up with it, 'They have got the name of this place wrong.' he said, 'Not Svans but crows. If only we'd brought a shot gun we might have been able to grab their attention for a minute.'

'Don't mention guns,' said Frank nervously. 'I think this place is bristling with arms already! But the knitting intrigues me,' he continued. 'They all seem to be knitting the same thing!'

We focused on the knitting, and Frank was right. The Svan

women almost all seemed to be knitting thick woollen socks-like garments but obviously with an eye to getting into the 'Guinness Book of Records' as to which of them could produce the longest.

'It can't be socks,' I mused, 'they are far too long. Scarves maybe?'

'Or maybe they are woollen scaling ladders,' Mitch said managing a smile, 'for when they attack each other's towers.'

'That was a most successful meeting,' trilled Tamuna as the Svans started to drift away to milk their goats, make their yoghurt and whatever else it is helps them live so long.

'They are obviously enthusiastic, as they always are here in the mountains. And now they want us to join their supra.'

'Will Lado be drinking at the supra?' Frank asked in terror, thinking about the hazards of the road home.

'Of course!' said Tamuna. 'We are not driving back down until tomorrow and we must not deny him the pleasures to be had here in the mountains. They have some very interesting brews up here, not to be found anywhere else in the world.

'Your Irish poteen should have you in good training for this!' laughed Mitch.

Toasting the Departed

'How did you make out last night at the supra?' asked Frank next morning. He had escaped the festivities by claiming the altitude was making him ill, a ploy that had nearly backfired on him for the hospitable Svans had a remedy for altitude sickness which had all the appearance of being yet another potent alcoholic brew. He had accepted this graciously, took it to his room, and thereafter would not reveal its fate to us.

'I think,' replied Mitch, 'that we should draw a thick Svanetian woollen 'sock' over last evening's supra. One thing: whatever their hooch is up here, it certainly helps you to forget! And it might just be that same hooch that helps them to live so long. You may have missed out there Frank!'

We started on our way down, Lado in decidedly over-confident mood.

'What happens if we meet anything on this road?' I croaked to Mitch.

'One of us goes crashing to oblivion,' he said philosophically. 'Don't waken me to tell me we have gone over the edge. I don't mind dying without knowing.'

We had been travelling for about two hours on this numbingly dangerous road, when something surreal even by Georgian standards happened! At a particularly fearsome hairpin bend, Lado pulled in and stopped.

'Oh please God,' I prayed, 'please let it be that even he can't take this road anymore, and we are all going to have to walk the rest of the way even if it takes us years.'

But no! Lado had got out to pay his respects at a little shrine by the road-side.

'Perhaps I should not tell you,' said Tamuna, 'but these shrines are erected to young Svan men who, sadly, did not make it home. Perhaps one small error on the road and...!' she shaded her eyes. 'Lado has stopped at this one – for I am sure you have noticed several such shrines along the road – because he knows this young man's family.'

I looked out of the window at Lado paying his respects at the shrine. But what was he doing? He was drinking something from a plastic bottle dangerously similar to the ones being passed round at the meeting yesterday, the same ones that had been filled with the local fire-water that had done the rounds at the supra last night! Surely I was seeing things!

'It is a tradition among our men,' Tamuna was reading my thoughts, 'that we toast the departed, as Lado is doing now. The family of the departed always sees to it that there are full bottles at the shrine where the accident happened. But do not worry,' she said reassuringly, 'Lado will not take much. A sip or two only.'

*A roadside memorial to
an accident victim*

The three of us were struck dumb! There was nothing to be said! I tried to comfort myself by thinking that many of our drinking customs in Ireland are just as ridiculous, but that was cold comfort on the road from Svaneti!

Flying or Driving?

'Ah, one never wants to leave Svaneti,' Tamuna was in poetic mode again. 'It is so close to Heaven, you never want to come down.' As Lado swayed his way back to the jeep, I could think of other reasons at that very moment why I didn't want to come down but I just shut my eyes.

'Does everyone travel up to Svaneti by road?' Frank asked Tamuna when ours had got slightly broader and less pot-holed, and we felt our breath coming back.

'Well, you can fly up to the capital, Mestia. It takes about an hour.'

'So why didn't we fly, Tamuna?' Everything American and logical in Mitch suddenly boiled over.

'It is not always convenient,' she replied. We had learnt

that Tamuna used the words 'not convenient' when what she meant was, 'I didn't want to'. 'You see, there are only flights on Mondays and Fridays, and even then the flight will not take off unless the plane is full and the weather in the mountains is suitable for landing, so travel there and back can be a little uncertain and can take several days. Also coming in to Mestia is through the high mountain passes, and the plane lands on a grass field, sometimes with cows around, and so it is not always flat or pleasant. And I have heard of refuelling problems,' she tailed off leaving us to ponder how lucky we were to be with Lado in the jeep even if he was a bit the worse for wear.

'What do you think she meant by "fuel problems"?' Frank pondered a little later. 'Does it mean they take off, run out of fuel and have to glide back to Tbilisi or is there no fuel at times in Svaneti, and they can't take off until fresh supplies arrive – in gas cans? If so maybe coming by road – even this road – is better than that,' he said, clearly trying to convince himself.

'Just think,' said Mitch, 'if we had flown, we could have been stranded up there for weeks. You would have got used to the altitude, Frank, and could have joined in their next supra!'

But Frank, staring out of the window into the latest yawning chasm, wasn't listening.

Mission Impossible

When we were about half way down to 'ground level', we came upon two young men standing by a broken-down jeep similar to ours on their way up to Svaneti. Lado stopped to see if they needed help. As he tinkered with the engine, we discovered the men were two Jehovah Witnesses from Ohio on their way, presumably, to try to convert the Svans!

'Oh dear,' said Frank, when Lado had got the young men's engine repaired and we had all resumed our journeys, 'I fear that if ever two men were on a "Mission Impossible", that is it! Short of a miracle, of course' he added.

'If there are any miracle going around, it's us that needs one on this bloody road,' said Mitch. 'Speaking of miracles and conversions, Tamuna,' he continued, 'how did the Svans take to

Communism in Soviet times?'

Tamuna thought for a moment and then smiling broadly said, 'I do not think the Svan's were very enthusiastic Communists.'

We had no trouble believing her!

'A Truly Awesome Part of the World'

St. Zacharias Icon. eleventh century. Museum of History & Ethnography of Svanetia

After what seemed like an eternity, we joined a better road and felt we could breathe again. Of course, people travel (indeed fly) to Svaneti, and do so in perfect safety. After all, Svaneti has been named a World Heritage site and even we in our tousled, semi-sober state could see why. It is a wonderful medieval landscape with its ancient towers, villages and churches backed by some of the tallest most spectacular mountains in the world, ever snow clad. And inside Svaneti's incense-filled churches hang some of the most beautiful ancient icons ever created, before which glow hundreds of candles. Inside the Svaneti homes too, a welcome so warm, so giving, so truly unforgettable as to tear at the heart strings of even three jaded Westerners like Frank, Mitch and me. The food in Svaneti is as distinctive as their language: at the supra we sampled kubdari (a delicious meat pie), chvishdari (a cheese concoction in maize bread) and various dishes based on cream, yogurt and honey. We each came away loaded down with presents of their fiery hooch and some of the long woolly 'socks' as mementoes of our unforgettable visit to this truly awesome part of the world.

'I suppose I could always insulate the loft with it back home' said Mitch trying to roll his 'sock' into a manageable ball.

'So where to next, Tamuna?' asked Frank.

Uncomfortable Hot Spots

'South Ossetia,' said Tamuna, 'but you will not come there. It is not entirely comfortable.' This was another of Tamuna's little phrases, the true meaning we had long since learnt to interpret. When she said we could not accompany the team to certain parts of Georgia because it was 'not comfortable' it meant 'still quite dangerous'. The locals had not yet been weaned away from encouraging Russian interference and the habit of taking pot-shots at their fellow Georgians. Visiting Westerners might get caught in the cross-fire or might even be kidnapped for ransom. Before we had set out for Svaneti, we noted that Tamuna had said that Svaneti used to be 'uncomfortable' but was now very 'comfortable' so it was reassuring that the Svan's had got over these bad habits. But South Ossetia and Abkhazia, Georgia's two disaffected regions, are still ones that pose problems for the government in Tbilisi, and offer attractive footholds for the Russians. Since they were 'not comfortable', Mitch, Frank and I could have a day off, and leave those particular consultation visits to our Georgian colleagues.

During our stay. Abkhazia remained out of bounds for all of us, even the Georgians, but South Ossetia was not yet entirely a 'no-go' region for Georgians. Coming from Northern Ireland with its reputation for being dangerous when, in fact, only certain areas were directly affected by the 'Troubles', I was emboldened to volunteer to go with my Georgian friends to South Ossetia, but they would not hear of it. So after the trip up through 'hell' to 'heaven' in Svaneti, I took a duvet day in bed; Mitch caught up with e-mails, and Frank wrote an article for his church magazine back home. In the event, the Georgians had no trouble in South Ossetia, and came back flushed with success.

'See how well they get on without us!' was Mitch's comment as we braced ourselves next morning for more Georgian-style meetings back in the Ministry.

Chapter 6

'Massacres & Sulphur Baths' – A Walk Through Tbilisi

Metekhi Church from the Old City Tbilisi

'Which of our massacres would you like to start with?'

'I want to take you for a walk through Tbilisi today. It will be a walk through Georgia's history. Which of our Capital's massacres would you like to start with?'

It was breakfast time on a Saturday morning, and it was Shota's voice at the other end of the phone. 'Tbilisi has been razed to the ground many times over the centuries so almost wherever we start our walk, it will be with a massacre.' Shota was a very bright, erudite young man who worked with our team in the Ministry from time to time, and my stunned silence, occasioned by the strangeness of this introduction to taking a walk, obviously puzzled him. 'Are you still there? I said you have a choice of starting point. Wherever we start we will take in Tbilisi's two main avenues, Chavchavadze and Rustaveli, and they lead into the Old City. We won't cross the river into the Metekhi district or go near your former hotel. You have already been accused of planning to shoot our President from there, so we will give that a miss.'

'About these massacres,' I said, ignoring Shota's mischievous reference to my embarrassing encounter with President Saakashvili's bodyguards early on in my stay, 'what do you mean, I have a choice?'

'Well, I could meet you at Sioni Cathedral down in the Old City,' Shota continued. 'That is the site of several of our greatest massacres,' he said, with a hint of something approaching pride. 'When we were invaded in the thirteenth century, it is said that Sultan Eddin found it entertaining to have the dome of our Cathedral removed, and have his throne placed there so that he could watch the citizens of Tbilisi being drowned by his troops in the river. Then in the early seventeenth century, the Persian ruler, Shah Abbas, killed 70,000 of us beside the cathedral in three days, and took 100,000 slaves. But, as you can see, somehow we are still here!'

Again I fell silent, and Shota seemed to take my silence to be reluctance to start our walk at the far end of Tbilisi from my new hotel.

'Or,' he said, 'we can start up there in the Vake District where you now live. Mind you, we will still be starting on the site of a massacre. Your present hotel and the whole of Vake are built over the graves of thousands of Beria's victims. You have heard of Beria? He was Stalin's henchman here in Georgia, and he had thousands shot during the Stalin purges in the 1930s, including most of the Georgian aristocracy and bourgeoisie.' After a moment's reflection he continued thoughtfully, '... though, of course, not all of his victims are buried under you there in Vake.' I think this was meant to console me somehow, and again before I could reply Shota continued, 'or I could meet you half way.' He was clearly determined to lure me out that Saturday. 'We could meet at our parliament building half way down Rustaveli Avenue, see the wonderful exhibition of Colchis gold across the road in our National Museum, and then walk down into the Old City.'

'Would that not be only half the walk?' I ventured, for curiosity to see everything he had mentioned was now getting the better of me.

'It depends,' said Shota. 'Are you bringing Frank and Mitch with you? You know how they complain if they are subjected to too much culture.' This was unfair. Frank and Mitch disliked anything that distracted them from work, but I knew what Shota meant.

'I'll ask them,' I said. 'But surely your parliament building isn't the site of a massacre?'

'Don't you believe it!' said Shota 'Twenty-two Georgians, including several women, were shot by Russian troops on the steps of the Parliament as recently as 1989. 'Oh, I think you will find our history is as violent and as bloody as yours in Ireland,' he said triumphantly as if we were in competition. 'It is because both our countries are so beautiful,' he continued, 'others have always wanted to take them from us.' He paused, 'And Georgia has also always been a crossroads between East and West, and much fought over because of that' he added in a way that seems to imply that this gave Georgia an even greater edge in the 'massacre' stakes.

While I pondered, Shota continued to throw a great deal more cultural and historical 'bait' into the call, for it could never be said of him that he was not tenacious or indeed that he wore his erudition lightly!

As well as the magnificent collection of Colchis Gold (of Jason & the Golden Fleece fame), I would see 'the three-thousand-year-old mud and sulphur baths where everyone from Alexander the Great to George Bush have taken the plunge, the Caravanserai where the camel trains rested in Old Tbilisi before crossing the river to continue their journey along the Great Silk Road to China, the seminary where the young Joseph Djugashvili (Stalin to us) had trained as a priest and the palace where he housed his mother when later he ruled half the world. It might even be possible to see Beria's house and his much frequented bedroom.'

He paused for breath and, taking my continued lack of response to be reluctance to join him, he then lowered the tone considerably by saying 'I will even take you to the Irish Pub down in the Old City. I hear it serves great Guinness'. Clearly he was determined to educate me that Saturday, whatever it took!

Far from being reluctant, I was very keen to go, but I had work to catch up on, and so had Frank and Mitch. However, I quickly salved my conscience by telling myself this was necessary cultural background for our work, and so agreed with Shota to start the walk in Vake Park near our hotel. I confess that until his call I was unaware of the existence of an Irish pub in Tbilisi so, what with the cultural feast before me and the prospect of this home comfort at the end of the walk, how could I resist!

But others could resist!

'What!' exclaimed Mitch, 'I have been fighting for weeks with the Ministry to have at least Saturdays off, so that we can catch up with the paperwork, and now you go and sign us up for a city hike.'

'But its culture,' I said. 'You surely don't want to leave Georgia as ignorant as when you arrived!'

'With Shota and you around, chance would be a fine thing,' Mitch muttered. 'And I know you are only going so you can find that pint of Guinness you have been hankering after for weeks.' I ignored this, but it was indeed in this mixed state of enthusiasm and with equally mixed motives that we met Shota in the hotel lobby and set off.

Vake Park

'First we will visit Vake Park,' he said. 'It contains our Museum of Folk Architecture where you will see reconstructed houses typical of all the regions of Georgia.' When we reached the Park, Shota was determined we would do the museum in depth. Mitch had other ideas, and was getting hot in more senses than one!

'Since we have so much to see today,' he said to Shota,

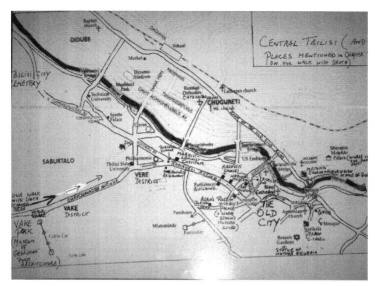

Map showing the route we took through Tbilisi

'couldn't we skip the houses that are typical of Georgia's two break-away regions, Abkhazia and South Ossetia?'

Shota glared at him in disbelief. 'But,' he said crossly, 'it is the houses of those very regions that you must see so that you understand how very 'Georgian' these break-away regions, as you call them, really are!'

Frank sensed a diplomatic incident in the making and said soothingly, 'We could skip seeing the reconstructed Svaneti towers since we have already seen those for real when we were up in Svaneti.'

'And anyway,' said Mitch trying to recover lost ground, 'we live so close to here, we can always drop by on our own, now we know there is so much to see in the Park.'

'OK,' said Shota, 'let's go and see a few of the more typical houses just to give you a flavour.' So we got a flavour, and very interesting it was too.

'Now,' said Shota when we had had a restoring coffee in the museum restaurant, 'let's stroll down Chavchavadze Avenue, and I will explain to you who he was.'

Example of a traditional Georgian house. Open Air Museum of Georgian Folk Architecture, Georgian Nationasl Museum, Vake Park, Tbilisi

Chavchavadze Avenue

Chavchavadze Avenue in the Vake District may be resting on one of Tbilisi 'killing fields' but is now the city's equivalent of Regent Street in London and Grafton Street in Dublin. Clearly there are an ever increasing number of Georgians who can afford the prices in the luxury shops lining the Avenue, more and more of which are opening by the week. Mitch cast his usual sceptical eye over all this as we strode along.

'I reckon a lot of this plush development is a way of laundering money,' he said. 'I'll bet the old cronies Eduard Shevardnadze brought back with him from Russia, and who plundered this place after independence, have invested their ill-gotten gains in all this real estate and consumer durables.'

Shota ignored this in best Georgian fashion, and attempted to raise the tone.

'Have you heard of our great author and poet, Ilya

Chavchavadze, after whom this Avenue is named?' he asked. We confessed we had not. 'He was one of Georgia's greatest early twentieth century novelists and poets, and a great Georgian nationalist, but he always voiced his hopes for our national and cultural revival in a voice of moderation.'

'How did he make out?' asked Mitch.

'The Russians assassinated him in 1907,' said Shota. 'Now why does that not surprise me!' said Mitch.

'I must take you to see his home outside Tbilisi,' Shota continued. 'We are hoping to turn it into a literary centre and venue for a summer school.' He paused and then continued, 'like your W. B. Yeats Summer School in Ireland. We have heard of this, and we all think Yeats and Chavchavadze have much in common. Both are near contemporaries, both were distinguished poets, and both were caught up in their country's national revival and struggle. What do you think?' he said to me, 'could a link be established between the two summer schools?'

Some weeks later, Shota did indeed take me to the Chavchavadze country house and, possibly because of the

Bust of the author, poest and Georgian nationalist Ilya Chavchavadze, assassinated in 1907

sumptuous supra he and his friends had arranged for me on the terrace or maybe because of the beautiful atmospheric house and gardens, I too came to see a distinct connection between Chavchavadze and Yeats that evening. Happily, one crucial difference between them was that Yeats was spared Chavchavadze's fate. On a dark winter's evening in 1907, as their car was approaching the house, Chavchavadze and his wife were ambushed and he was killed, the very spot now marked with a sombre monument.

'And now here is Tbilisi University,' said Shota, pointing across the Avenue. 'Isn't it a distinguished building?'

'It is distinguished,' muttered Frank, 'as Universities usually are these days by that crowd of layabouts hanging out on the front steps.'

I think Frank's feet were already getting sore from the walk.

Rustaveli Avenue

'This is where Chavchavadze Avenue merges with Rustaveli Avenue,' declared Shota, 'and here,' he continued with noticeable pride, 'is the statue of Georgia's very greatest literary giant – Rustaveli himself!'

Shota Rustaveli. twelfth century Georgian national poet

'And there is a McDonald's,' exclaimed Mitch, 'and it's time for lunch!' There is now indeed a recently sprouted McDonald's restaurant towering – literally, since it actually looks like a glass tower – over the statue of Rustaveli. The shape of things to come in Georgia!

Shota ignored Mitch's call to dally in the home of the 'Big Mac' and said hopefully, 'Of course, you will know who Rustaveli was?'

'Twelfth century?' I ventured, 'Treasurer at the court of Queen Tamara? Greatest of all the literary figures Georgia has produced?' I looked to Frank and Mitch for help, but they both now appeared to be fixated on McDonald's.

'Good,' said Shota generously, 'but let me fill in the details. Rustaveli was indeed Treasurer at the court of one of our greatest monarchs, Queen Tamara, in the twelfth century. He is our Shakespeare. His most famous work is 'The Knight in the Panther Skin' which was translated into English in the early twentieth century by the Englishwoman, Marjory Wardrop. She is still a great heroine here in Georgia for undertaking that work. But her translation, though generally good, has certain errors due to the fact that she taught herself Georgian by comparing words in Georgian and English Bibles.'

'You don't say,' said Mitch. 'She must have had lots of time on her hands.'

'It was a great labour of love,' Shota continued. 'She knew how much Rustaveli's great poem meant to Georgians, and she wanted to make it known in the West. Is it widely read in the West?' he asked hopefully. Before we could answer (or at least think of something to get us off the hook) he continued 'Georgian children learn great sections of the poem by heart, and brides in Georgia receive a copy of it on their wedding day.'

'Just like back home,' said Mitch with a straight face, 'where brides get a copy of the Complete Works of Shakespeare!'

We wandered on into Rustaveli Avenue with all our hopes of a Big Mac and French fries fast receding.

Statue of Georgia's 12th poet Rustaveli facing the McDonalds 'Tower' in Rustaveli Avenue, Tbilisi

We were now passing a very grand building on the steps of which artists were selling paintings and other souvenirs, and which Shota explained had been a royal palace when Georgia had a king.

'Was that built before or after your king handed Georgia over to the Russian Tsars at the end of the eighteenth century?' Mitch asked pointedly,obviously in revenge for his disappointment over the Big Mac.

'There were good reasons for the Georgian King seeking the protection of the Russians at that time,' Shota said, clearly trying not to let Mitch get to him. 'We were in danger of being over-run by the Turks, but sadly the Russians did not honour their treaty with us, and we simply became part of the Tsarist Empire. The rest is history, as you say in English.'

'That building over there,' he said pointing to one with enormous columns on the other side of the Avenue, 'that was the Marxist-Leninist Institute in Georgia in Soviet times. There used to be busts of Marx, Lenin, Engels and Stalin up there,' he said pointing to plinths near the roof, 'but they were removed and smashed to pieces on the street below when the Soviet Union collapsed and we got our freedom.'

'What did the Communist guys do in there all day in Soviet times?' asked Frank.

'They foisted Moscow's foolish centralised policies on us here in Georgia, one of which – their "command" economic policy – almost ruined us. But all that is behind us. As you can see, the building is now empty and looking for new tenants.'

The former Marxist-Leninist Institute, Rustaveli Avenue, Tbilisi

'It would make a good home for your Ministry,' said Mitch. 'I can see it now – instead of those busts of Marx and the other guys, you could have busts up there of Tamuna, Nana, Eka, and you Shota.' We stood looking at the former Institute for a few moments, and I couldn't help thinking of the power, now consigned to history, it once wielded over the lives of Georgians. With its firmly bolted doors, blinded windows, and four empty plinths where the effigies of the Communist leaders had once been, it spoke volumes for the death of big ideas.

Beside it stood Tbilisi Opera House, 'rebuilt in the Moorish style after the great earthquake and fire of 1870,' Shota explained. On this side now was Prospero's English bookshop and cafe with the alluring smell of coffee. We succumbed, collapsed at a table, ordered coffee, and took stock!

'You Georgians have had one hellava time of it,' said Mitch as we sat on Prospero's terrace drinking our coffee, with the Union Jack fluttering above us from the adjacent British Council offices, 'what with Stalin and Beria massacring you, your literary guy Chavchavadze being shot just as he was getting you all warmed up about nationalism, then the crazy ideas imposed on you from that Marxist Institute place and, on top of that, these darn earthquakes that shake you up now and again. How have you managed to survive it all?'

'Oh,' said Shota, 'you haven't heard the half of our history. We have been invaded so many times – by the Persians, Byzantines, Arabs, Turks, by Genghis Khan and his Mongols, by Tamerlain, and then there was our usurpation by the Russian Tsars followed by the Bolshevik Revolution and the horrors of the Soviet period,' he broke off to see if we had taken all this in. 'How have we survived? Simple! We are Georgians!'

'I see,' said Mitch obviously impressed. 'Some outfit! You know, I now think you might even survive us!'

'This is our Parliament Building,' said Shota when we resumed our walk down Rustaveli Avenue, 'and the site of our most recent massacre.'

We sat down on the steps of the Parliament looking across Rustaveli Avenue to the beautiful Kashveti Church of St George opposite and, beside it, an open space with hoarding round it.

'Over there,' Shota was pointing at the empty space, 'that

Georgia's parliament building and the monument to the citizens massacred in 1989, on Rustaveli Avenue

was where the beautiful Artists' House once stood, but it was destroyed by the bombardment during our Civil War in 1992. And on these very steps where we are sitting, 22 peaceful Georgian demonstrators were shot by Russian soldiers on 9 April 1989, stung into such barbaric action by our declaration of independence. They continue to punish us for our new friendship with the Americans. They are doing all in their power to frustrate our efforts to join NATO and the European Union. 'But, as I said, we are Georgians! We will endure, and we will triumph in the end! Now come and look at the memorial to the Georgian martyrs who died on these steps in 1989, for they died for Georgia and for our freedom.'

When we had paid our respects at the simple moving memorial, Shota said 'Let's cross the road to visit the National Museum and to see the Colchis Gold, for it was to Georgia, or Colchis as our country was then called, that Jason and the Greek Argonauts came in search of the Golden Fleece. You must know this legend?' It was clear that, as the walk progressed, Shota was increasingly taking less and less for granted about what we knew. 'An Irishman called Tim Severin reconstructed Jason's ship the *Argo* and sailed it from Greece to Georgia to prove that the story of Jason and the Argonauts may have been true, and that they did indeed come here in search of the Golden Fleece. Have you seen the programme about Severin's journey on television?'

I assured him that I had, and he seemed a bit happier.

'As I recall the programme, it was a terrible journey,' I said, 'but it seemed to prove the legend may have been based on fact.'

'Never mind this Jason guy and his problems getting here,' said Mitch, 'how are we to cross the road in this traffic?' How right he was! The standard of driving in Georgia is appalling, and no better in central Tbilisi than anywhere else. However, following Shota's courageous lead, we ventured forth, and somehow got to the other side of Rustaveli Avenue safely.

'I have made arrangements for you to have a guided tour by one of the Museum's most knowledgeable curators and an expert on the Colchis Gold,' he said, looking pleased with himself.

Janashia State Museum, Rustaveli Avenue, Tbilisi. Part of the Georgian National Museum

The curator – a formidable woman – greeted us briskly, and led us down a flight of steps into the Museum Treasury.

'It is a pity you have not got time to see the whole of our museum collection,' she said, 'we are a very ancient nation reputedly descended from Noah.'

'Oh yes?' said Frank with interest, 'didn't Noah's ark come to rest on Mt Ararat?'

The guide smiled, 'Yes,' she said, 'in the land of our neighbours the Armenians, but it is of course only a legend.' I could see that Frank was disappointed by this comment since he believed the Bible story, and the lady herself seemed torn between wanting to ground the Georgian nation in the loins of Noah and her training as a scientist to question such stories. By now we had arrived in the Museum's Treasury, and so began our very memorable museum tour. Beautifully decorated golden lions, stags and horses from three thousand years ago, solid golden bowls decorated with amber, lapis lazuli and cornelian, gold necklaces, chains decorated with golden birds and turtles, and hairpins inset with garnets and agate, the most wonderfully crafted rings, tiaras, pendants, and ornamental broaches, and so much more.

See colour plates 1 to 7 for the museum exhibits

'What kind of stone is cornelian?' asked Mitch, clearly much impressed by what we were seeing.

'It is a semi-precious stone which was much used in jewellery in ancient times since it was considered to ward off the "Evil Eye",' explained our guide.

'Some of these gold bracelets remind me of torques that are displayed in our museums in Ireland,' I mused. The curator quickly turned a gimlet eye on me!

'And what age are they?' she demanded. 'You should know that the objects you are looking at here are among the oldest gold ornaments ever found anywhere!'

After that rebuke, I felt I sorely needed a lump of cornelian to save me from the 'Evil Eye.'

The display was beautifully arranged. Our guide explained that the little gold lion, which displayed the most remarkable craftsmanship and had come to be something of an emblem of the collection, dated from 2600 BC. She pointed out a bowl which was also set with cornelian, and which dated from 2000 BC.

Some of the most stunning exhibits had been excavated at Vani in the west of Georgia near the Black Sea coast, and were particularly interesting historically because Vani was thought to have been the city ruled by King Aetes to whom Jason and the Argonauts had come in search of the Golden Fleece.

'Looking at all this gold,' Frank mused, 'it is quite believable that Aetes owned any number of golden fleeces.'

'Our ancestors specialised in a distinctive form of gold decoration,' our guide continued, determined to educate as well as impress us. 'They chose a granulation technique using tiny lumps of gold to create this unique texture. These beautiful gold horses, which were used to decorate horses' harnesses, are good examples of the technique. Are they not exquisite? They are so delicate, they can only have been used for ceremonial purposes.'

'And here we have a beautiful necklace and earrings, made in the fifth century BC, also in the city of Vani, which demonstrates the granulation technique particularly well. Aren't the little gold turtles on the necklace amusing? We believe they were symbols of longevity for the people of those times.'

'But I think this little fellow really is my favourite,' she said, pointing to a rider whose horse was strangely fitted out with wheels. 'These are the most delicately wrought earrings, again crafted in Vani in the fifth century BC. Wouldn't your wife or girlfriend be happy if you took these home to her as a gift from Georgia? And here are the fourth century BC brooches to match them,' she beamed on us as we gazed in awe at the exhibits, clearly delighted that we were so impressed.

'Now come to the next room,' she said, leading the way. 'In here is still more Colchis gold ornaments and artefacts but to fully appreciate the intricate detail of these exhibits, they are displayed under special lighting. Come, you will see for yourselves.'

And indeed we did, for these delicate and exquisite Colchis gold objects were displayed on softly lighted blue velvet cloths in an otherwise darkened room, and they radiated the wealth, splendour and craftsmanship of a very distant age.

Back on the street, Shota drew our attention to a lovely building on the same side of Rustaveli Avenue as the Parliament building.

'That was the Russian Governor's Palace in Tsarist days,' he said, 'and then it was where Stalin installed his mother in the 1930s. But the old lady could not get used to the grandeur. She was, after all, used to living in a one-roomed house above her husband's cobbler's shop in Gori, so she cut and ran back to end her days there. She was called Katerine, or Keke for short, and she never wore anything but black, and insisted on shopping in the market herself even when she had to be accompanied by her NKVD bodyguards. She had always wanted Stalin to be a priest;

indeed she never tired of telling him that he should have stuck to being a priest every time they met, but clearly his destiny lay elsewhere! He did start training for the priesthood in the seminary just round the corner from here. Come and see,' and he set off at a brisk pace.

Rounding the corner where Rustaveli Avenue merges into Pushkin Square, we found Shota striding up the steps of yet another beautiful building.

The Art Museum of Georgia in Tbilisi and former Orthodox Seminary where the young Joseph Stalin was a student priest

'This was the seminary where the young Joseph Djugashvili – or Stalin to all of us now – trained for the Orthodox priesthood,' he explained. 'It is now our main Art Museum. You must come and see the wonderful Pectoral Cross worn by Queen Tamara, the medieval icons and, of course, the collection of Pirosmani's paintings. You have heard of him? He was our greatest artist of the twentieth century.'

'But what about stopping for some lunch, Shota?' pleaded Mitch.

'We Georgians only eat when we are hungry. You are surely

not hungry yet? You Americans must learn to feed the mind before the stomach!'

'I think that comment qualifies as being literally "below the belt!"' said Mitch, trying to laugh and not look too annoyed. Shota, realizing that his remark had apparently given offence to the otherwise thick-skinned Mitch, said quickly 'We will eat when we get to the Old City which is close by, but now you must see the wonders of this Art Museum,' and he led the way to the ticket desk. This irregular eating is a feature of life in Georgia. Our Western notion of punctuating our day with regular meals seems not yet to have caught on, and you can order the most elaborate meals in Georgian restaurants at the oddest times, and get freshly cooked food even if you are eating 'lunch' at four o'clock in the afternoon in a largely empty restaurant.

The Art Museum on Pushkin Square was yet another wonder. We admired the beautiful medieval crosses and icons set with precious stones and worked in enamel, and, as Mitch said wryly 'were probably best seen fasting'. And of course there was the cross of Queen Tamara which was also a reliquary said to contain a fragment of the True Cross. We paused in front of it for some time. To us foreigners, it is remarkable because of its age and associations but it was clear that to Shota and Georgians it is much, much more. This object is a symbol of all that their country has been and might again become – united, respected, prosperous, distinctive, Orthodox – just what Tamara's ancestor and Georgia's other great monarch, King David the Builder, had striven for, and Tamara herself had finally achieved in the late twelfth century.

'To think,' said Shota, 'that she wore this cross all her life, and that the great Rustaveli himself would have seen it daily, just as we are seeing it now. The Queen was the inspiration for much of Rustaveli's literary work, you know, and there are unmistakable references to Tamara in his "Knight in the Panther Skin".'

Hungry and footsore as we were, we too lingered before Tamara's cross and then before those other great symbols in the Museum, the fifteenth century Icon of St George, so often copied and also so charged with meaning and hope for all Georgians, and the magnificent eleventh century triptych of Our Lady of Khakhuli, the largest cloisonné enamel in the world.

See colour plates 8 & 10

And so upstairs to see the Pirosmani paintings.

'Is this called primitive painting?' asked Frank.

'"Naif" is a better description,' said Shota. 'Aren't they charming? It is a pity that some are away on loan for you are not seeing Pirosmani's full range.'

'Shame.' said Mitch, and then to me out of the corner of his mouth, 'it's a pity my grade school teacher didn't keep some of my paintings when I was seven. If she had, I might have been as famous as this guy.'

'Sadly much of his work is lost,' continued Shota. 'You see he was not appreciated until it was almost too late.'

See colour plates 11-15

Beria's Big Bed

We crossed Pushkin and then Freedom Square, where workmen were in the process of erecting a statue of St George to replace the one they had removed of Lenin, and, to repair relations between Mitch and Shota, had another cup of coffee and some cake in the rather grand Tbilisi Courtyard Marriott Hotel. Thus restored, to some extent in every sense, and back on the Square again, Shota led the way up a leafy side street paralleling Rustaveli Avenue. He stopped in front of a long elegant house with a narrow garden in front.

'This is where Beria lived,' he said, 'while he was in charge of Stalin's many purges during the Terror in the 1930s here in Georgia.'

It looked like an eighteenth century gentleman's gracious town house, and it was quite impossible to imagine the horrors that were planned behind its windows, as Beria systematically terrorised Georgia into submission and silence on Stalin's behalf.

'You promised us a glimpse of Beria's bedroom,' said Frank, who was a stickler for keeping people to their word.

'It used to be possible to see inside the house before it was taken over by the Ministry that is now based here, but I think it has all been altered to accommodate the civil servants. I have seen his bed,' Shota added. 'It was enormous for such a small fellow. But then you will know that he was very active in bed, and that his NKVD bodyguards, who were also his pimps, kidnapped young girls for his pleasure. Many of the girls committed suicide afterwards, they were so ashamed.'

'Nice fellow!' said Frank, and then in a moment of unusual passion he added, 'I hope Beria is not still up there with Stalin as a hero in Georgia?'

'No, Beria is not well regarded by anyone,' Shota assured him, 'and while some Georgians still have a high regard for Stalin – "a strong man when strong men were needed" they will tell you – that is very much a minority view in Georgia now. Personally I think Stalin was a monster.'

'Yes I think having the death of millions of people on your hands would qualify you as a monster,' said Mitch with more than usual sarcasm.

Shota pondered this for a moment, and then said 'I suppose, when you think about it fair and square, it is not only we Georgians who are a little ambivalent about Stalin. You will know that he was Britain and the USA's ally during World War II, and there are historians who would argue that the West would not have defeated Hitler without his help.'

This trip through history was getting deeper by the minute! We strode thoughtfully into the Old City.

'Now,' said Shota, 'I may have failed to show you Beria's bed, but I will not disappoint our Irish friend over something far more important – that pint of Guinness. Round the next corner is Tbilisi Irish Pub.'

It wasn't like any Irish pub back home, but it served good draft Guinness which was most welcome and which, in best Irish and Georgian fashion, kept coming, so we emerged a little later than intended to explore the Old City.

The Old City

The Irish pub was close to a sort of crossroads at the heart of the Old City district, and perhaps it was the Guinness (or the Coke in Frank's case) that had us a bit disorientated but I found myself looking down at the river Mtkvari, and the Metekhi bridge crossing it which had carried the Great Silk Road linking Constantinople to China. There too under the shadow of Metekhi Church, and the equestrian statue of King Vakhtang Gorgasali, who founded Tbilisi in the fifth century, were the beautiful houses with their balconies overhanging the river.

'This really is a beautiful city,' I said.

'But look this way,' said Frank pointing back the way we had come. 'Look at these quaint houses with their balconies and vines, and the washing hanging out, showing they are real and lived in by honest-to- God people. It is so wonderful to have seen all this before the planners get here!'

'Well, they have got here,' said Mitch pointing towards the fourth century AD Persian Citadel on the hill above us, 'and they are not making such a bad job of it. Surely you guys agree it is good to see all this American investment being put to good use?'

In a way, we had all got it right. The Metekhi bridge and Church is a medieval and a magical sight. The Old City is mysterious and atmospheric but still lived in and so is not a museum, and the renovations in progress under the Citadel are as sensitive as they are necessary if the whole place is not to fall down. But, as Frank had said, it is a privilege to have seen Tbilisi before it increasingly comes to look like everywhere else.

See colour plate 19

Sioni Cathedral

We reached Sioni Cathedral, which is both at the heart of the Old City and also the heart of Georgian Orthodoxy in Tbilisi. It was from the Sioni tower that the Sultan had witnessed the drowning of many of Tbilisi's citizens in the thirteenth century. We entered the cathedral to see the fourth century cross of St

Nino, the Cappadocian slave girl who had converted Georgia to Christianity. The cross was difficult to see in its elaborate shrine, but what was just as interesting was the crowds of teenage Georgians crowding the church to take part in a service which was underway. It confirmed to us yet again that Georgian Orthodoxy strikes a deep chord both in terms of religion and nationalism, and is once again a very potent force with the youth of Georgia.

When I mentioned this to Mitch later he said 'Unfortunately yes, for increasingly it is anti-American.'

'How come?' I asked.

'Because,' he said, 'our American fundamentalist religious sects flooding this place are luring too many young Georgians away from the Orthodox Church with offers of free education in their schools and places in their colleges back home. Is it any wonder the Orthodox are getting mad at us! Already the powers-that-be here in Georgia have had to banish some Orthodox priests and monks to some remote monastery somewhere because they are preaching against the American presence in Georgia. But you wouldn't know anything about powerful priests, would you, coming from Ireland!'

The cathedral was rich in ancient icons, with worshippers, young and old, praying and lighting candles before them. In the midst of the throng, we spotted Shota waving us over to see one particular icon which turned out to be that of a man who had a modern appearance.

'This is Georgia's latest saint,' whispered Shota. 'It is Ilia Chavchavadze. I told you about him this morning as we walked down the avenue named after him. Remember I said that as well as being a great author and poet, he was also a great Georgian nationalist. That is why he is now honoured also as a Georgian saint.'

I reminded Shota of the comparison he had made earlier between this man and our W. B. Yeats. 'Back in Ireland, our man is not a saint yet,' I laughed, but it was clear Shota didn't see the joke.

1. *Gold earrings, fourth century BC*
Janashia Museum of Georgia, Tbilisi: Georgian National Museum

2. *Gold brooch with garnets, Vani, fourth century BC*
Janashia Museum of Georgia, Tbilisi: Georgian National Museum

3. *Gold necklace with turtles, fifth century BC*
Janashia Museum of Georgia, Tbilisi: Georgian National Museum

3a. detail

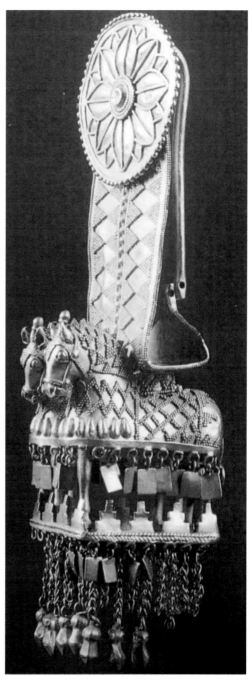

4. Gold ornaments for horse's harness, fourth century BC Janashia Museum of Georgia, Tbilisi: Georgian National Museum

5. Gold lion from a funeral chariot, third millennium BC

6. Gold bowl with inlaid cornelian, lapis lazuli and amber, 2000-1500 BC
Janashia Museum of Georgia, Tbilisi: Georgian National Museum

7. *Gold earrings with horsemen, Vani, fourth century BC*
Janashia Museum of Georgia, Tbilisi: Georgian National Museum

8. Icon of St George
gold, cloisonné enamels
Art Museum of Georgia, Tbilisi:
Georgian National Museum

9. Pectoral cross of Queen Tamara
late twelfth to early thirteenth century
Art Museum of Georgia, Tbilisi:
Georgian National Museum

10. Our Lady of Khakhuli triptych, eleventh century
10a & 10b details
Art Museum of Georgia, Tbilisi: Georgian National Museum

11 to 15. Examples of Niko Pirosami's art

16 to 18. The tomb at the fortress monastery of Ananauri and its forgotten thousand-year-old frescoes of the life of Christ

19. View of Tbilisi from
the heart of the old city

20. Fresco of the Angel
Gabriel in the church at
Atenis Sioni
painted in 1080, it
represents a high point in
Georgian art

'People need martyrs, saints and poets to raise their consciousness as a nation,' he said sharply. 'I have read your history, and I think no Irishman could disagree with that.'

'Here is the Caravanserai,' said Shota stopping before a renovated building next to the cathedral. 'This is where merchants have congregated, rested their animals and done deals from the earliest times. However the present building dates back only to the early nineteenth century and now contains the Museum of the History of Tbilisi. We will give it a miss and go straight to the Baths.'

The sigh I heard to my left was unmistakable, and it wasn't one of disappointment!

Naked as Nature Intended!

We walked along the river looking across at the beautiful balconied buildings overhanging the cliff face, then scampered across the road to the square around which are grouped Tbilisi ancient hot sulphur baths.

'I think you would be happiest in the Blue Baths,' said Shota pointing to a building at the top of the square which was ornamented with blue tiles and white minarets.

'What does he mean "happiest"?' said Frank anxiously. 'I've heard the bathing here is naked, and I'm not up for that!'

'Take it easy,' said Mitch. 'I'm sure you won't see anything you haven't seen before! Stay cool man!'

Staying 'cool' wasn't that easy! When we entered the baths, the clammy heat from the hot springs and the overwhelming smell of sulphur nearly drove us out again. But we persevered. Shota was already at the reception desk negotiating our entry fee, having assured us that they would charge more when they realised we were foreigners and didn't understand the system.

'Now,' he said, 'do we want a private bathroom or will we use the public baths?'

'Oh public,' said Mitch, 'nothing like experiencing life in the raw, eh Frank?'

Frank had the look of a man about to flee, but before he

could do so, we were all laden down with towels, soap and large shapeless sandals.

'Now remember,' said Shota, 'you can only use the baths naked, nothing else is acceptable.'

Frank's worst fears had been realised! 'Tell me there are no women in there?' he croaked, and it wasn't just the sulphur affecting his throat.

'No,' said Shota, 'women come on Tuesdays and Wednesdays.' Thus reassured, we entered the changing rooms and stripped off.

'I have paid for a full massage for all of us,' said Shota disappearing into the bathing area. In the self-conscious way of naked westerners, we too entered and, to hide our embarrassment, quickly plunged into the nearest hot sulphur pool.

'This natural water comes from the depths of the volcano on which Tbilisi is sitting, and is millions of years old,' Shota said, determined to impress us with everything about his native city.

Now that we were less conscious of the sulphur smell, and with the other bathers not taking the slightest notice of us, less self-conscious too, the experience was turning out to be very enjoyable. The water was soft, even oily, on the skin, and the atmosphere very relaxed.

Until the masseur appeared! He was grim-faced, muscle-bound and Russian, and he was taking no hostages! He crooked a finger at the four of us, and Mitch went first. He was thrown on a marble slab and 'attacked' from every angle for about twenty minutes. Then a Hessian sack was produced filled with some kind of detergent, and he was pummelled with this to within what looked like an inch of his life. This was followed by another severe beating, as we watched cowering below the parapet of the sulphur bath. The final assault on Mitch involved what appeared to be a dance performed on his back with a large pair of Russian hands and feet. Mitch returned to us battered but unbowed, and even smiling! Then it was my turn! By the time the mighty Russian had dealt with all of us, the sweat was literally rolling off him, but he had doubtless done us proud! We left the baths walking on air. I never felt better in my life!

'That was just what we all needed after the long walk from Vake, and your day-long encounter with Tbilisi and our history,' said Shota triumphantly, 'and believe me there is plenty more to see. You have not explored the Persian Narikala Citadel up there on the hill, or seen the statue to 'Mother Georgia' with her sword in one hand to defend Georgia and her bowl in the other to offer Georgian hospitality to strangers. But speaking of hospitality, I think you are now ready for a good Georgian dinner!'

So to a Georgian restaurant a few steps back in the Old City. There, beside Tbilisi's ancient synagogue and under the gaze of King Vakhtang Gorgasali, we met up with some of Shota's friends and spent the evening gorging on items from the sumptuous menu. We shared lamb with tarragon and plums (chakapuri), salmon buglama, duck with walnuts (ikhvis chakhokhbili), Georgian meatballs (abkhazura), kidney beans stewed with coriander (lobio), potato pancakes (labda), cooked cheese with mint (gadazelili khveli) and stuffed aubergenes and tomatoes, all accompanied with plum, walnut, and blackberry sauces and bottles of rich red Mukhuzani wine, white Tsinandali wine smelling of peaches, and Georgia's own mineral water from Borjomi.

And so to bed! We fell out of the restaurant and into a taxi to take us back to our hotel at Vake. What a day! What a history lesson! What a wonderful city! What a place this Georgia is!

Chapter 7

The Lively Corpse

'None of you are outsiders now!'

Eka rang one morning to say that Nana's grandfather had died suddenly, and that all team work would be on hold until after the funeral. Frank, Mitch and I were, of course, keen to offer our sympathy but had no idea of the proper procedures in this most family orientated of countries. How could we find out? I rang Eka back.

'He will be brought back to Nana's home and will be honoured there by relatives, neighbours and friends for three days, then there will be the funeral,' she explained.

'How can we, as outsiders, show proper respect for Nana's grandfather and our concern for Nana?'

'You can visit her house, and then attend the funeral like everyone else,' said Eka simply. 'Anyway, none of you are outsiders to us now, but our good friends and colleagues.' I felt a lump come to my throat, and I suddenly felt very homesick. This was so like how bereavement would be dealt with back in Ireland when people still take time to give the really important matters of life and death their proper due.

'The funeral is in three days time, and tomorrow afternoon we are to attend the 'wake' as we would call it back home,' I explained to Frank and Mitch.

We arrived at Nana's home at mid-afternoon. There was a crowd on the pavement which turned out to be the tail end of a sort of queue snaking its way up several flights of stairs to Nana's apartment, all folk wishing to pay their respects. Others who had already done so were coming down the stairs on the right hand side, as we joined the queue going up. Unfortunately we found ourselves behind our dreaded rivals who were serving in one of the other teams in the Ministry.

'Trust us to get behind those smart asses,' said Mitch. But there was no ignoring them, and we all pretended to be glad to see each other.

'Keep them off the subject of work,' warned Frank as we approached them. 'I had the misfortune to have dinner with two of them the other evening and, by comparison with us, they are going great guns.'

'I sincerely hope you didn't tell them the truth about our efforts,' Mitch was bristling, 'surely for once Frank, you could have lied.'

'I said we were 'on target' which I thought was safe enough since we don't have any targets that I've ever noticed.'

'Oh, well done,' said Mitch, '...and you remember that!' he said turning to me, 'We are on target if the subject comes up.'

It didn't come up; what came up instead was the subject of death. 'This is dreadful for poor Nana,' said Kauko, an earnest high-powered Finn, whose only saving grace was that every now and again he got roaring drunk, 'especially after the recent death of her mother too.'

Frank asked Kauko if he knew the age of the deceased. 'He was well into his eighties I heard,' replied Kauko.

'Well, that was a good age,' said Frank, 'and if he was prepared and ready...' he faltered uncertain how to go on since clearly the deceased would not have been 'born again' in Frank's terms..... 'and I always think that it's not so bad when the elderly go first. It's in the natural order of things,' he finished lamely.

Kauko looked at him scornfully, 'But surely you are furious with death,' he said with great intensity. 'Think about it – all that individuality, uniqueness, experience, hope, fears – all snuffed out in an instant. And what are we left with? A spoonful of ashes!'

'But we go on to a better life if....' Frank's evangelical enthusiasm was cut short because by now we had arrived at the door of the apartment. The queue proceeded down a narrow hallway into the living room where the remains lay in his coffin dressed in his best suit and surrounded by tall burning candles.

Two Orthodox nuns and a priest were in attendance, and relatives and friends sat around the coffin. Knowing that Nana was unlikely to have eaten anything, and well aware of her passion for sweet things, the ever thoughtful Frank had brought a box of biscuits which he left beside her chair. It was at that moment that we lost Frank who went on to have a strange and unnerving adventure on his own. He told us about it that evening.

Frank's conversation with Kauko had left him trailing a little behind the rest of us in the queue, so he was the last to offer his sympathy to Nana. She appeared grateful for his sincere concern for her, and indeed for the biscuits, and had said to him,

'Please don't go just yet. You are, I know, a devout Christian. It was so very kind of you all to come.'

Frank's Heavenly Trance

The room was very crowded, and Frank eventually found a chair which, by chance, was very close indeed to the deceased. Feeling a little uncomfortable, he sat down and found himself beside a very old lady dressed in deepest black. The priest and nuns were continuing with the beautiful Orthodox liturgy for the dead as the long queue of mourners continued to circulate around the coffin, some stopping to kiss the remains, all shaking hands and embracing Nana and her family, very many in tears. Frank soon felt privileged and moved to be there, and his earlier feelings of intruding vanished. The heavy scent from vases of large white lilies, the sweet scent from the flickering beeswax candles and the smoky incense from a burner held by one of the nuns combined to lull Frank into a sort of trance. He gave in to it, but was suddenly brought back to consciousness by a jolt which appeared to have come from the direction of the remains.

'The Corpse is Moving!'

Surreal thoughts flooded in! Had he too died, and had he and the remains gone to another place, and was this resurrection day? Or was the man not dead? Was he indeed about to get up! Frank snapped out of this uncharacteristic reverie to be once again scared out of his wits by yet another and louder creak from the deceased. Nobody else was paying any attention even when there were further odd sounds from the coffin followed by a noticeable shudder. Frank tugged the shawl of the old lady beside him since she had now heard the sounds too and was looking lovingly at the corpse.

'What?' Frank stuttered, 'What is happening? Is he moving?'

'I suppose I really meant to say, "What are we to do?"' Frank explained to us later.

'Ah,' said the old lady calmly, 'look how well he is settling.'

Frank knew when he was out of his depth so he made his excuses and left. Mitch, who now claimed he had worked in a funeral parlour when he was a student, proceed to tell us that a corpse 'settling' for some time after life has departed is not that unusual, and would have regaled us with similar strange facts on death and corpses but Frank and I assured him we had heard enough.

'You haven't actually committed murder!'

'You should not have taken Nana a present!' We were travelling to the funeral with Eka, and Frank had just told her casually about the biscuits.

'When a Georgian family is in mourning, they do not receive gifts and certainly not any kind of food for they are fasting, and the idea that any kind of gift would comfort them at such a time is….' she paused trying to let poor Frank down lightly '…not in our traditions.'

'I suppose I should have asked about your mourning customs before I did it,' Frank was mortified as only you can be when you meant well by some action, but it has turned out badly. 'I will apologise to Nana'.

'Oh, don't worry about it,' said Eka, and then inadvertently added insult to injury by saying, 'it would be worse if you had murdered somebody.'

Slow Marches and Fast Hearses

We arrived outside Nana's apartment block just as the remains were being borne out of the front door unto the street. The open coffin, followed by the mourners, was then carried very solemnly and slowly to the end of the street where it was put into the hearse. Given the quiet dignity and slow solemnity of the occasion so far, what happened next was surprising. The hearse set off at breakneck speed through the Tbilisi traffic followed by the mourners who had piled into cars. Several times we lost sight of the hearse entirely, but fortunately Eka knew which cemetery it was going to so we finally caught up with it as it was going through the gates. Then began another hair-raising journey for the roads through the cemetery were like dirt tracks and heavily rutted so that at times the car seemed in danger of turning on its side. However, we were not so much worried about ourselves as the remains in the coffin in the hearse ahead of us.

'How on earth are they keeping the remains upright?' mused Frank. 'Faith alone,' said Mitch. 'Surely you should know that, Frank!'

We finally arrived at the area of the cemetery that was located on a high hill overlooking a beautiful steep valley, with the suburbs of Tbilisi in the distance. The grave was at the very edge of the slope into the valley, but there was still no path from the roadway to the grave. Once again the coffin was lifted high and borne over many other tombs to the open graveside. There it was laid down, and close family and friends gathered round to say their last farewells. The family were, of course, greatly distressed and repeatedly rearranged the deceased's clothing in the open coffin as if making him comfortable in bed. There was no priest present at this final committal, the religious ceremonies having been completed back at the apartment, so the family took complete charge. When the final embraces were complete and the deceased made thoroughly comfortable in his coffin, the lid was placed on it and it was slowly and lovingly lowered into the grave. All the while, several elderly women dressed in deepest black and swathed in heavy shawls wept and lamented loudly around the grave in a way which in Ireland long ago would have been called 'keening' for the deceased.

As we were making our way back across the graveyard to the car, walking over graves and slithering round headstones nearly all of which had pictures of the deceased person engraved on them, I noticed that most also had a stone or iron table beside the grave. I asked Tamuna what the table was for. She explained that forty days after the burial, the family return to the grave and have a meal in honour of the deceased. Often families also return on certain anniversaries, birthday, or Saints' Days to have a picnic at the graveside, laying the food and wine out on the graveside table.

'It is our way of remembering our loved ones who have departed and keeping them part of the family,' she explained.

'Sort of graveside supras,' I ventured.

'Yes,' said Tamuna, 'and speaking of supras, you are all now invited to the family's supra in honour of Nana's grandfather. All the preparations have been made and it will be held in a hall nearby.'

The Funeral Supra

We were a little embarrassed to arrive at the hall before most of the chief mourners but were, as always, made warmly welcome, and found four long tables stretching the full length of the large hall, laid out for the funeral supra and already laden with food and wine.

'A lavish funeral supra is a tradition in Georgia,' Eka explained. 'You know that we are very family orientated as a nation, and it is regarded as very disrespectful if a relative, friend or indeed acquaintance of the deceased does not attend the funeral. Many come a great distance – Nana's grandfather lived for most of his life in the country so many people at his funeral today will have travelled from his part of Georgia, and so must have a meal before they set off for home again. That has always been our way in Georgia, in good times or bad, but I sometimes think the food is too lavish and elaborate especially for families that cannot afford it, though that, of course, is not a problem for

Nana's family. However, the honour of the family is at stake for all Georgians on such occasions so a great funeral supra must be provided come what may.'

And so it was that afternoon. We were seated opposite a number of men who had come from the deceased's village, and who looked as though they had stepped out of a Pirosmani painting. As delectable dish followed delectable dish and toast followed toast in best Georgian fashion, we became quite chummy with the countrymen even though we didn't speak a word of each other's language. Eka explained the toasts as they were proposed by the Tamada, a relative of the family, and which were a little different in style at this more sombre funeral supra. She also explained the dishes that I didn't already recognise, one of the most delicious of which was 'sweet porridge' which, Eka explained, traditionally ends a funeral supra.

A Country Supra. Niko Pirosmani 1862-1918

With the sweet porridge served and the toasts completed, we offered our sympathy and thanks once again to Nana and her family, and returned to our hotel. Most of the Georgians present showed no signs of leaving, and were obviously setting down for an evening's socialising just like an Irish wake.

As we drove back to the hotel, Mitch said, 'I have never been to a funeral where the deceased actually played such an active part'.

'Oh please don't remind me of corpses moving or settling,' said Frank with a visible shudder.

Chapter 9

Through the Valley of the Devil to the Gates of the Alans

Magic Moments, Sick Cows and More Supras

'A sick what?' I asked.

'Cow,' said Andreo, 'or maybe it's a horse. Anyway Georgi has to attend to it before he takes us to the meeting. He says it will not take long.'

My young driver and guide on this occasion was Andreo, and he and I were in the High Caucasus on the border with Russia at the historic mountain pass called the Gates of the Alans, and instead of addressing a meeting at the scheduled time, I appeared to be about to help with a sick cow! I consoled myself that I have had plenty of practice with cows back home on the farm in Ireland; maybe it would all come flooding back.

'But Andreo,' I said, 'are we not going to be late for the meeting in Kazbegi. Won't the folk there get impatient?' I still hadn't got the hang of the Georgian way of doing things, least of all their attitude to time keeping.

'No, no,' Andreo assured me, 'they will understand about Georgi's cow and how important it is for him to attend to that first. And anyway, we can't go to the meeting without him. He has to introduce you and translate for you.'

Georgi was indeed the lynch-pin in these parts – farmer, translator, Ministry official, ad hoc vet, and, we were to learn, driver extraordinaire of the little four wheel drive Russian 'Niva' that could take you up near vertical mountain slopes.

Soso Strikes Again!

My unsought adventure at the Gates of the Alans had started one Monday morning when Tamuna, at her normal start-the-week briefing, got into an uncharacteristic panic.

'We will have to split up,' she declared. 'Soso says we need to speed up the consultation exercise and cover more ground more quickly.'

Casting a doubtful, troubled eye over Frank, Mitch and me, she said, 'You are all now very experienced and know what has to be done. Do you think you could conduct some of our consultation meetings on your own?'

Perhaps because we looked dismayed – instantly calling to mind some of the sessions we had already witnessed – or maybe we just looked blank, Tamuna continued, 'I mean,' she said, 'each of you will take a meeting on your own, as we Georgians will also be doing. We will provide drivers and interpreters, of course, but we must all now go our separate ways if we are to complete the consultation in time … that is Soso's decision,' she finished as unconvincingly as she always sounded when she called upon the elusive Soso to back her up.

'Where had you in mind for each of us?' asked Mitch, as Frank and I tried to put a brave face on what lay ahead.

'Oh, you will only go to areas where we expect a very positive reception to our plans,' Tamuna assured us, obviously determined not to discuss this any further or hear any objections. She continued quickly, 'Frank, I think you could go and speak at the meeting in Kakheti in Eastern Georgia, and Mitch, I think you can cover the consultation group at Batumi on the Black Sea. And you,' she said turning to me with a disarming smile, 'You I will send up the great Georgian Military Highway to the Gates of the Alans in the High Caucasus.' This sounded as daunting as it was dramatic, and in the same histrionic mode, Tamuna continued, 'There I know the Irish will triumph where even the Roman General Pompey failed to conquer, at our impenetrable Caucasian Gates on our border with Russia … and with Chechnya!' she added with a hint of mischievousness.

And so it was that I was dispatched to the Gates of the Alans in the High Caucasus at the end of the Georgian Military Highway which had been built by the Russians in the nineteenth century, and appeared to have not been much repaired since.

Andreo's Long-distance Love Life

Frank, Mitch and I had long since decided that drivers in Georgia regard driving as an art and not a science, and my friend from the Ministry and driver on this occasion, Andreo, was typical of the breed. To him, obeying traffic lights was optional, the right and left side of the road a matter of whim, and speed of the essence. My nerves were already on edge before we had got to the outskirts of Tbilisi, but by the time we got to the Pass of the Cross in the High Caucasus we had already survived so many near misses, I was calmly fatalistic. I could partly understand Andreo's maverick road discipline since he often had to take to the wrong side of the road for nerve-racking stretches to avoid enormous potholes on his side, but did he have to keep calling friends on his mobile as we literally teetered on the brink of yawning chasms? There were few protective barriers and, as soon as we had taken up position on the wrong side, a Georgian version of 'Murphy's Law' kicked in, and hurtling toward us would come equally kamikaze drivers often in old Soviet-style lorries with undoubtedly dodgy brakes.

Back with the never-ending mobile calls, Andreo appeared to be having a domestic crisis for his mobile rang about every five minutes and occasioned an ill-tempered spat down the phone, and much dark muttering in Georgian when the call ended. I was later to learn that these calls were from his girlfriend, and were the unlikely birth-pangs of his proposal of marriage but I was not to know that at the time. Every time his mobile call-sign went – which for some reason was 'I'll take you home again Kathleen'– I gritted my teeth and hung on to the door handle. The higher we got into the mountains the worse the road surface became and the more Andreo had to pull across to travel on the wrong side. He explained to me, between telephone calls, that the dreadful road surface was not entirely the Georgian

Ministry's fault. Frequent landslides, enormous mud slicks, avalanches, earthquakes and the simple if alarming fact that these gigantic mountains are still 'babies' and are still 'growing' at some astounding rate every year all make their mark on the surface of the Great Highway.

We hit the Highway at Georgia's beautiful ancient capital and religious centre, Mtskheta. I closed my eyes as Andreo, overtaking everything in sight, took the Georgian driving art form to new heights of derring- do, and I just consoled myself that, anyway, this was a very Georgian expedition! What with the bad road surface for long stretches, the apparently bottomless chasms often on both sides of the road, the disaffected region of South Ossetia to our immediate left, smouldering Chetnya somewhere to the North, and the fact that, even if we ever got there, the Russians, in a bloody-minded moment, had closed the Gates of the Alans to all but 'approved' traffic, why should I worry. Placing myself once again in the hands of Fate, I settled back to enjoy the magnificent scenery.

As we followed the valley of the river Aragvi north into the Caucasus, still snow clad even in the height of summer, Andreo's love life appeared to be reaching some sort of crisis – or was it a conclusion? As I sat waiting for the next shrill burst of 'I'll take you home again Kathleen', I never knew that I hated that tune so much. I was torn between desperately trying to remember the words, now that I'd told Andreo it was an Irish song, and wanting to grab his mobile every time the tune rang out, and hurl it through the window. In a very sporadic way, between these highly charged phone calls, Andreo gave me bursts of information about the history of the Military Highway. He explained that the road has been the main highway into Georgia from the north for up to three thousand years. At first it was only a bridle path, then was fashioned into a more recognisable road by Georgia's great king, David the Builder, in the early twelfth century, and finally widened and paved by the Russians when the then King of Georgia, Irakli II, handed the country over to Orthodox Russia for protection from Georgia's Islamic neighbours in 1783.

'Who are the Alans?'

'Very many famous people have travelled this road,' Andreo continued. 'It was at the Gates of the Alans that the Roman General Pompey had to abandon his conquest of Asia.. In the nineteenth century, the famous Russian writers Pushkin, Gorky and Tolstoy, and the French author, Alexander Dumas, have all written about coming through the Gates of the Alans, some in vile weather, and then travelling on down the Military Highway to Tbilisi. We are more fortunate; the weather for our journey is so beautiful today.'

His mobile rang again, and the tussle of love continued call after call, punctuated by that hated call-sign. When there was a slightly longer pause than usual between calls, I took the opportunity to ask Andreo about the Alans, and what exactly are their Gates? He explained that the people who live in and around the town of Kazbegi, to which we were now bound and which is besides the Gates of the Alans, are descended from the Alan Tribe. They were great fighting men who from time immemorial had guarded Georgia's northern frontier. The so-called 'Gates' are where the Military Highway enters the very narrow Daryal Gorge and runs high above the river for about twelve kilometres, with very steep cliffs on both sides, up to the border with Russia at the Devil's Bridge.

'It is spectacular and a bit frightening,' Andreo continued. 'Before the coming of air travel it was the only land route through the Caucasus to and from Georgia. We Georgians still regard the Gates of the Alans as our Northern Gate.'

We travelled on up this beautiful valley with the mountains gradually closing in on each side. Ahead of us I could see a long narrow lake shimmering in the summer sun, and at the top of the lake a fortress-like building with several towers.

'Saints Alive!'

'This is the fortress monastery of Ananauri,' said Andreo reading my thoughts, and screeching to a halt when we reached it. 'Come, I want to show you something wonderful that few have ever seen!'

Ananauri resembled a small medieval town with several churches with pepper-pot towers contained within its walls, now all deserted and in decay. Andreo led the way down a narrow path between the monastery walls and the lake until we reached an entrance gate. We made our way to one of the less dilapidated of the churches and, as my eyes became accustomed to the darkness inside, I could dimly make out a large tomb to the right of the central isle with a massive stone canopy soaring over it. Andreo produced a torch from his pocket and shone it on the inside of the tomb's stone canopy.

The deserted fortress monastery of Ananauri
on the Georgian Military Highway

'Look up,' he said.

At first, all I could see was graffiti in Russian scrawled on the lower half of the canopy, presumably the work of bored soldiers stationed there over the centuries to guard the Military Highway. But then above this, on the over-arching dome of the canopy itself, and just out of reach of all but the most determined graffiti artists, was the most wonderful sight. There in the torch light were vivid and magnificent frescoes depicting scenes from the life of Christ – the Nativity, Baptism, Crucifixion – all painted on the canopy of the tomb over a thousand years ago.

By this time, Andreo was obviously missing his mobile so he handed over the torch and left me alone with the frescos. In the dim light, I experienced a kind of epiphany for I sensed for the first time how men and women in the Middle Ages must have felt as they entered their local church. Until the Puritans whitewashed over them, the walls of most of the churches of Christendom were covered in vivid paintings like this, and to those men and women, the great majority illiterate, the pictures meant everything. They would have entered the church, even more dimly lit by candles than this tomb's canopy by Andreo's torch, and it must have been easy to believe that the saints and martyrs covering all the walls and ceilings were actually present and worshipping with them.

See colour plates 16-18

Andreo reappeared, and we resumed our journey north. By way of thanking him for taking me to see the frescos, and in an embarrassed self-conscious way, I tried to explain to Andreo what I had sensed back in the semi-darkness of the tomb.

'I think I understand,' he said, showing far more interest than I had expected. 'You know we Georgians were all officially atheists in Soviet times. Young people especially dared not show any interest in religion if you wanted to get on, but our Grandmothers told us what they knew about the Christian Faith, and now my friends and I go to church again. We are learning to be good Christians – Georgian Orthodox Christians,' he added correcting himself, 'for a good Georgian must be Georgian Orthodox! Your experience back at Ananauri interests me,' he continued, 'when you saw the saints come alive. My Grandmother used to say that when you enter an Orthodox church you have stepped out of time and into eternity. So you are not alone; you are worshipping God together with the holy saints and martyrs who are already in Paradise. My Grandmother is still alive. I will tell her of your vision at Ananauri. She will understand it better than me for I am only learning to be Orthodox.'

His mobile rang again. This time it was his mother to ask him something which resulted in yet another acrimonious shouting match down the phone, and the spell woven in the church was broken. Still, I will never forget Ananauri and its lively frescos!

The Devil's Valley

We were now above the snowline, the surface of the Georgian Military Highway was steadily getting worse and worse, and Andreo's driving was even more fast and furious, and mostly on the wrong side of the road to avoid the craters. Occasionally he swerved to avoid disappearing down long, ominous looking avalanche tunnels designed for vehicles to shelter in if drivers got any warning that mountainsides of snow were on the move and heading in their direction.

'Look there,' said Andreo, with his mobile yet again in one hand, and his other hand off the steering wheel and pointing, 'that is the cross erected by King David the Builder in the twelfth century to mark the top of the Pass. That is why it is called the "Pass of the Cross", and now we enter the "Valley of the Devil".'

I had just time to glimpse a large cross at some distance from the road jutting out of the snow away to our right before Andreo said, 'The cross on this side,' he was now waving his mobile in the direction of another cross to our left, 'that was erected by the Russian General who supervised the widening of the highway in the early nineteenth century.'

'Let's stop, so that you can look down into the "Stone Chaos" from the viewing platform yonder.'

Andreo was heading for a horseshoe structure which, he told me, had been built by the Soviets to mark 200 years of Russian/ Georgian 'friendship'. One look at its present state of decay was proof positive that the friendship was no longer close for the monument had clearly been left to fall down. Pieces of the mural depicting 'Soviet Motherhood' and another 'Soviet Youth' were lying on the ground inside the structure, and other propaganda-laden heavy slabs looked as though they might fall on us at any minute.

But this danger was nothing to what awaited us out on the viewing rail. The decaying platform looked down into an abyss so

The Soviet-built viewing platform overlooking the 'Stone Chaos' in ther High Caucasus

deep and terrifying it must surely be one of the unacknowledged wonders of the world. Eagles and vultures swooped and dived well below us reminding us that, at this height, we were out of our element as mere mortals.

The Niva near the Gates of the Alans in the High Caucasus

Back on the road again, even Andreo had to slow down to avoid the boulders and deep ruts that had now became a feature of the Highway. After about an hour of dodging and ducking these obstacles, Andreo pointed ahead. 'We are almost there,' he said. 'The pass ahead of us is the Gates of the Alans… and the Russian frontier.'

So we had made it, and here was the town of Kazbegi. Now to find Georgi, the local 'Mr Fix- it', he of the sick cow!

Georgi resembled a down-to-earth farming man anywhere, and would have passed unnoticed in any Irish country town on a market day. I confess I am not sure what I expected since we are all 'Caucasians' whether we live in Ireland in the West or the Georgia Caucasus in the East. He understood that I was anxious to get to the meeting, but explained that his cow must be attended to first. We all piled into his little Lada Niva and took off to find the cow. It was fortunate that the Niva itself performed like a mountain goat for once again the mountain tracks quickly became almost vertical. The first obstacles we had to get around were the livestock wandering in the town of Kazbegi itself. A pig blocked Georgi's way near the centre of the town, and moved only when it was good and ready despite much honking of the Niva's horn, and then we ran into a large herd of sheep which nobody seemed in any hurry to move on.

With these living obstacles behind us, Georgi revved up the Niva, turned off the Military Highway and took a rough track

The 14th century Church of the Holy Trinity, Kazbegi

into the mountains.

Up and up we went, with Georgi screeching to a halt only to lift the bigger boulders that were strewn on the narrow track. In the far distance was a beautiful old church silhouetted against snow clad Mount Kazbegi.

Prometheus Bound!

'That mountain is where our Georgian Prometheus is bound,' Andreo shouted above the roar of the little Niva's toiling engine.

'That's right,' said Georgi raking through the gears, 'he stole the fire from the Gods and gave it to us mortals so he has been tied ever since to Mount Kazbegi. You can clearly see his shape in the mountain there.'

The air at that high altitude, the occasional swig of vodka from Georgi's flask, the jolting and shuddering of the Niva all combined to put me in the frame of mind to believe anything so I thought I could clearly see the shape of a giant on the snowy mountain side behind the dark mysterious church.

'Why are so many of your churches built in such remote places?' I shouted to both men as we roared past this one.

'For security,' Georgi shouted back. 'Georgia has been invaded so often our churches either had to be built like fortresses or built in remote places like this. Either way they had to be nailed to the ground to survive. And they have survived,' he said triumphantly 'and so has Georgia!'

He now swung the Niva into a narrow valley where the track was at last flat and level. I was just beginning to appreciate the superb scenery when a young lad on a horse suddenly appeared from nowhere. In my disorientated state, I wouldn't have been surprised if it had been Prometheus himself but it turned out to be Georgi's son. He told his father that the cow was near the 'falls', wherever that was, and that she needed urgent attention. Georgi revved up the Niva, clearly all thoughts of our meeting back in Kazbegi out of his mind. We followed the lad on the horse into a rolling mountain meadow where Georgi abandoned the Niva and sprinted across a wide, very fast flowing stream that we all forded by jumping from loose boulder to loose boulder.

In the process, I got my feet very wet, and wondered vaguely how I was ever going to address the meeting back in Kazbegi, if I ever got to it, with wet feet? The horse and rider were now far above us on much higher, boulder-free ground, but Andreo and I had to follow Georgi through prickly scrub and over large boulders which he leapt like an Olympic athlete while we puffed and blew and panted to try at least to keep him in sight. We finally rounded an enormous boulder and found Georgi and son and sick cow in front of us. But to our amazement, forming a backdrop to the scene was the most spectacular waterfall cascading over a sheer cliff thousands of metres above us and tumbling into a deep dark ravine. It was a stunning sight, and it drew Andreo and me towards it by its power and majesty. It was another magical moment, and it cast an indelible spell in that remote lonely place.

We were both awakened from the enchantment by a gust of wind that enveloped us in a soaking spray. I was now soaked literally from head to toe, but I was past caring. Soaking or otherwise, meeting or no meeting, I wouldn't have missed the journey here and these magical moments for anything, and I knew they would live with me forever.

Meanwhile back with the cow, Georgi and son were triumphant! Nothing was broken, and it was not as bad as they had feared. They carefully tended to her and she soon ambled off, bellowing loudly, in the direction of the other cows. Georgi came across to join us at the falls.

'You like my waterfall?' he cried above the roar of the torrent. 'Is it not like a small Niagara? If it was nearer the road, I could sell tickets to travellers to come and see it, but here the climb is too difficult. Maybe when I am a rich man I'll build a chairlift from Kazbegi to my falls! But I almost forgot. We must get you to your meeting!'

I looked at my watch and I looked at Andreo.

'Are you sure the folk won't have given up and gone home?' I ventured.

'Nonsense!' said Georgi crossly. 'I promised them a supra if they were prepared to wait. You'll see! They will still all be there.'

Supras and Meetings don't Mix!

And indeed they were! The only problem was that they hadn't waited for the meeting to start or finish before getting down to the supra. The windows of the hall in Kazbegi were alight when we arrived, and inside the tables were already laden with the usual delicious food and wine and vodka. What about our meeting? How will we ever stop them eating, drinking, toasting and singing to get it going now? I still held on to the weird Western notion that work should come before pleasure!

'Don't worry,' Georgi put a reassuring hand on my shoulder, 'I will take your papers and translate them later and give them to everybody. They would prefer to learn about what Tbilisi has in mind for them in that way.'

Not at all reassured, I entered the hall and the supra. Here were some high Caucasus delicacies as well as the more usual Georgian fare, and I sampled khabajini (a potato form of khachapuri) and the very best khinkhali (dough envelopes here stuffed with pork) that I had tasted anywhere in Georgia. There was much toasting of all the usual 'suspects': St George, Georgia, mothers, Ireland, me as the special guest speaker though I had yet to say a word! I suppose some kind Alan must have escorted me back across the square to the Kazbegi hotel but I do not recall who or how. I met up with Andreo at the foot of the stairs and we crawled up them together.

'What will I tell Tamuna about the meeting that never happened?' I whimpered. 'Do you think we could hold some kind of short meeting tomorrow so that I have something to report?'

'Oh no chance,' said Andreo slurring his words. 'Tomorrow is the Feast of St. Nino who brought Christianity to Georgia in the fourth century. We will have to go to church. And don't you remember, Georgi said you can't leave Kazbegi without going on to see the Gates of the Alans, and then his farm in Sno Valley. But that will be after we attend church in honour of the Saint, and then, of course, there is the Saint's supra to follow. Don't refuse to attend!' he added quickly. 'A year ago a friend of mine brought some Yanks up here and they said they hadn't time to attend a supra so some of the locals shot up his tyres and the supra lasted on and off for nearly two days until the new tyres arrived. Its true! My friend wouldn't lie, not about something as important as his tyres ! We Georgians take our hospitality very seriously, you know!'

'As if I didn't know by now,' I moaned as I tried to focus on the handle of my bedroom door. I had to try to give the impression I was still in control of something!

St. Nino and Man. United

The Feast of St Nino dawned bright and clear which in no way reflected the way I was feeling. But in best Irish fashion I braced myself for another bout of hospitality Georgian-style in the High Caucasus. After breakfast, Georgi arrived and we set off in the Niva to the service which was in the little church we had passed yesterday set against the snow of Mount Kazbegi. By now I was good at keeping my head, sitting tight and holding on, as Georgian drivers and their vehicles negotiated bends, precipices and chasms that I had only ever encountered in nightmares. We arrived at the church – which Andreo explained was fourteenth century and was dedicated to the Holy Trinity – in its breathtaking setting, and went inside. Like much else in Georgia, it is well nigh impossible to be late for a Georgian service since they seem to have no beginning or end which I suppose is only to be expected if, as Andreo had told me earlier, they really represent Paradise on earth. The chanting of the priests and monks in that otherworldly place and its otherworldly mountain setting was my second medieval experience that trip, and it too has haunted me ever since.

What haunted me there and then was the prospect of another supra, but there was no escape! When there was a lull in the service, Georgi caught me by the sleeve and the three of us left the dimly candlelit church for the bright sunlight outside. A crowd of men, women and children had beaten a retreat from the service too and were lining up behind a large icon which I took to be St Nino. The procession moved off in the direction of

Mount Kasbegi singing, chatting and laughing. Where on earth were they going? Were they all going to climb the mountain? Was this a pilgrimage to some holy shrine above the snowline? Then light dawned! The women were carrying baskets of food, the men raw meat on skewers, the children bottles of wine and musical instruments. We were all supra bound!

'It is a barbecue supra,' said Andreo reading my mind. 'Look. Someone has lit the fires already,' and he pointed to a narrow glen leading away from the church up into the mountain. 'What a great morning we will have!'

And how right he was! Fires burned in the glen, mutton kebabs were prepared by the men, slices of Georgian meat loaf were distributed by the women, delicious cheese breads were shared around, toasts proposed, songs sung, and wine consumed in considerable quantities in the traditional rams horns.

Two small boys approached me as I sat on a large boulder beside the stream seeking sanctuary from both the feasting and the sun. Clearly someone had told them this was an opportunity to practice their English.

'Do you live London?' asked the tallest boy.

Before I could answer, they started whispering together, and the oldest boy asked what they both obviously really wanted to know.

'Do you support Manchester United? Do you know Wayne Rooney? We have picture of him at home in bed.'

I think I knew what they meant!

'We must go,' said Andreo. 'Georgi wants you to see the Gates of the Alans.'

Amid much beseeching us to stay, we piled once more into Georgi's Niva and set off down the slopes of Mount Kazbegi in the direction of the 'Gates of the Alans'.

A Glimpse of the Alans' Gates

'I hope my friend is on duty,' said Georgi, 'otherwise you will not see the pass. The Russians are only letting what they call essential traffic through at present, and they certainly don't welcome sightseers.'

We followed the river down a steep valley with the mountains closing in on us like enormous menacing pincers, made more ominous still by the massive ruins of ancient fortresses on every side.

'Oh good,' said Georgi, 'here is Demetri. I knew he would not let me down.' A man darted out from beside a ramshackle building which I assumed was a customs station outside which was a very long line of old Soviet style lorries waiting for permission to enter the pass.

'We can take the Niva a bit further, but then we will have to walk the last stage,' said Georgi. 'Follow Demetri, do not take photographs, and try to look like a Georgian going into the pass to do some maintenance work.'

'Pity we didn't bring our shovels,' said Andreo in a moment worthy of Mitch.

We drove on for a short distance, then walked for about half an hour, rounded a corner, and there before us were the historic Gates of the Alans. The valley had become a narrow gorge the walls of which looked a kilometre high, and along one side ran the road high above the thundering Terek River before both river and road disappeared into Southern Russia. I stood looking at the sight, and could see at once why travellers, past and present, had been awestruck by it, why the Romans had considered it the end of the known world, and why it had stopped so many conquering armies in their tracks. Through this narrow formidable pass have come, over three thousand years, royalty and plain folk, armies and merchants, authors and poets – some, like Pompey in his day and the Nazis in ours, to be halted in their tracks, some to trade, some to murder and rob, some, like Tolstoy, Pushkin and Dumas, to write, and to fall in love with Georgia. Never an easy passage in any sense, the Gates of the Alans have always been a front line between nations and cultures, and are so still today. This is surely one of those places on earth where history and geography collide.

'That's it!' said Demetri just audible above the roar of the river far below 'Your friend from Ireland has seen all that we can show him of the Gates of the Alans in these dangerous times. Now we must go back.'

Wolves and Bears

We arrived at Georgi's farm which was a little to the north of Kasbegi in the beautiful Sno Valley. On the way, I had spotted a magnificent chair lift which had obviously once linked the town to the Church of the Holy Trinity high up on the mountain, but the chairlift had been allowed to fall into disrepair.

'Why has that been allowed to happen?' I asked Georgi. 'It would be such an easy way to get to the church.'

'We Alans don't want it,' said Georgi with feeling. 'The Russians built it. We will get to our church in our own way!'

Georgi proudly showed us round his farm until well into the afternoon when Andreo seemed to be having the Georgian version of a panic attack. His mobile had been silent for quite some time, and I had lost touch with the twists and turns of his long-distance love life. Whatever the reason, he suddenly seemed keen to get underway. As we said our farewells to Georgi and his family, I noticed enormous metal braziers suspended on long poles dotted around the farm house and out-buildings.

'What are those?' I asked, pointing to the two positioned on each side of his entrance gates.

'We light them in winter,' said Georgi. 'They keep hungry wolves and bears at bay.'

Well, at least that is one thing the farmers back in Ireland don't have to worry about!

As we turned away from the Gates of the Alans, Kazbegi and Sno Valley, Andreo seemed to be in an even greater hurry than usual. The explanation was soon forthcoming and it did not fill me with great enthusiasm!

Wetting the Baby's Head

'We must get back through Devil's Valley and the Pass of the Cross before nightfall,' he said.

'Oh, I understand,' I said, 'the Pass and Military Highway will be so much more dangerous in the dark.'

Andreo looked at me scornfully, 'No, it's not that,' he said, 'I have just remembered the date. A friend of mine has had his first baby son, and he and some mates are having a supra to celebrate. They have come up to a hotel on the Highway at the village of Gudauri on the other side of the Pass. We are invited to join them.'

'That's great,' I said, my heart sinking at the thought of yet another supra so soon after the last two, 'but if we go we will not get back to Tbilisi today.'

'Then we will get back tomorrow!' said Andreo in best Georgian fashion. 'We will stay the night in the hotel, though I don't think we need rooms. We will not be sleeping much!'

The hotel in Gudauri was obviously well used to catering for a group of young men out for an evening's celebration. The management had wisely laid out the supra tables in a kind of underground cavern which, though directly below the hotel, must have been soundproof. When we arrived the supra was in full swing, with about twenty young men in various stages of inebriation arranged in various postures around a long table sighing with the usual supra fare. A three-man band was playing on a small platform, and some of the young men were dancing together in Georgian fashion while others took turns at joining the singer on the stage to help him with his songs. It seemed to be a great moment for them when they were told I was from Ireland, and after I had drained the Georgian wine from the ram's horn circulating round the table, Andreo and I had a bit of catching up to do in the toasting stakes. We duly toasted the new baby, his mother, father, family, his Homeland, my Homeland. That prompted requests for an Irish song! I manfully resisted Andreo's suggestion that I should sing 'I'll take you home again Kathleen' and instead gave yet another drunken rendering of 'Danny Boy' which got by because nobody was really listening.

'Dance! Dance! Irishman Dance!' and I was hauled unto the floor to be instructed by one of the young men how to do something resembling Cossack dancing. Several others gathered round to clap and cheer.

The supra to wet the baby's head at Gudauri
on the Georgian Military Highway

'Irish and Georgian people know how to enjoy a good supra – yes?' said my dance instructor, summoning up what English he could muster in the middle of the dance floor. 'Georgia good country; Ireland good country. Ireland and Georgia should be friends – yes?'

'Yes,' I said, 'Georgian and Irish people should be great friends.' I had obviously struck the right note. The young man shouted something to the others who were encircling the two of us, and they immediately rushed forward to slap me on the back and give me a series of bear hugs. Then, to my alarm, some of them grabbed me by the arms and legs and threw me up in the air three times! Then more hugs and back slapping, and I knew I had become an honorary Georgian at least for the evening. After that, the supra continued at full tilt. From time to time in the course of the night other young men would bond with me by trying out their English.

'Ireland,' said one, clearly trying to dredge up what he knew about us, 'you know Roy Keane – yes?'

'Did you enjoy your trip up Our Military Highway?' Andreo asked me when we finally got back on the road next day.

'Very much,' I said, 'but Andreo, what am I going to

tell Tamuna about the meeting at Kazbegi?' I was suddenly overcome with Western anxiety.

'Tell her ... tell her it went well,' he said. 'Well it isn't a lie,' he continued smiling, 'I mean it didn't go badly so it must have gone well.'

'But it didn't go at all,' I said, 'and I am sure Frank and Mitch will have lots to report to her. How am I to get round this without lying to her?'

'I've told you! Tell Tamuna the Alans seemed happy with what is proposed.' If I remember that evening correctly, when we left they all seemed very happy – about everything! And tell her Georgi will fill in the details.'

'That line of logic is worthy of us in Ireland, Andreo,' I said.

'Whatever you say, say nothing!'

Back in Tbilisi, I was mightily glad to discover that I was not the only one with much to conceal from Tamuna. It had been an ill-considered moment when she had sent Frank into the very heart of Georgia's main wine growing region, Kakheti. His session had got off to a bad start when the locals had tried to make him feel at home by having a supra before the meeting. They had not taken kindly to Frank's scruples about alcohol and his reluctance to drink when the toasts were proposed, for they saw this as a slur on the quality of their wine. After that, the meeting had been up hill and Frank's presentation had been greeted with stony silence!

Mitch had not fared much better on the Black Sea coast. The province of Adjara had only recently rejoined Georgia after a period of estrangement, and it soon became clear to Mitch that the good Adjarians were still of a mind to pick and choose what bits of Tbilisi's writ they would accept. The few who turned up to the meeting seemed mainly to have come to object to everything in principle even before they had heard the proposals in any detail. Mitch, never one to force the issue, and with a strong survival sense, had cut his losses, retired to a restaurant to eat a delicious local concoction called agaruli, and had then gone for a swim in the Black Sea.

'We must look on the bright side,' said Tamuna at the meeting next day. 'At least they have all heard our proposals, and that is a start.' She looked across the table at me.

'Georgi telephoned to say your meeting went well in the High Caucasus, and that you have cemented Georgian/Irish relations there. I knew the Irish and the Alans would get on well together!'

'So the only meeting that went well was the one that never actually happened,' muttered Mitch. 'What can we call that but the "luck of the Irish"!'

Chapter 9

Close Encounters with
Stalin's Bed and Bathroom

The statue of Stalin in Gori Central Square

'She is taking us to see what?' exclaimed Mitch.

'She said to tell you that you would see Stalin's bed and loo,' I said.

'We'll translate that into American as 'bathroom, and anyway, I don't believe it!'

Tamuna had just rung to say we were off up country again.

'We are going to a Conference Centre at Batumi,' she said. 'You know, where Georgia's excellent mineral water comes from. It is a beautiful spa town quite near the Turkish border high up in our southern mountains.'

'I don't like the "high up" bit,' said Frank. 'Did you ask her if there are any passable roads?'

The work had been especially hard and quite productive lately, and Tamuna had decided we needed a spot of rest and relaxation.

'We will revise and edit some of our recent papers,' she said, 'but nothing too demanding. You can relax at Batumi, sample the mineral and spa water, walk in the woods, and…' she had paused and added mysteriously, 'you may get to lie in Stalin's bed … and use his bathroom! Lado will call for you tomorrow morning. We must make an early start. The roads to Batumi are not very good in parts.'

'Oh brother!' said Mitch, 'sounds like the hike up to Svaneti all over again!'

Lado called for us next morning looking very pleased with himself.

'We can get some good cheap vodka on the way,' he said, 'and then we can have a proper supra at Batumi. And the spa water will clear away all hangovers.'

'What is all this about Stalin's bed?' Mitch asked Tamuna when we were underway.

'You will see when we get to the conference centre,' said Tamuna, 'just be patient. But before that you must see Stalin's birthplace. Our first stop is in Gori, the town where Stalin was born. There you will see his family home and the museum that contains some of his belongings.'

The Gory Man from Gori

'So he was born in Gori,' muttered Mitch. 'somehow seems an appropriate name for the birthplace of a mass murderer.'

'Gori means "hill" in Georgian,' explained Tamuna, deciding to ignore Mitch's asides as she frequently did.. 'The town is centred on a large hill on which there is a very ancient castle but we will not have time to see that – only the Stalin memorabilia this visit.'

We had all been intrigued by the Georgians' attitude to Stalin or Joseph Djugashvili to give him his proper Georgian name. 'A strong man when strong men were needed. Another Stalin is what we now need in Georgia,' a guy in a restaurant on Rostaveli Avenue had told me one evening, and then scolded the world in general for not appreciating what Stalin had done for all of us by helping to defeat Hitler.

'You hypocrites in the West forget that you owe your freedom to Georgia's great Stalin! He won the Great Patriotic War in 1945 for all of us.'

The colleagues we worked with in the Ministry were well aware of the suffering Stalin and his henchmen had inflicted on the Soviet people and on Georgia in particular, but they too were noticeably muted in their criticism. When his name came up, any criticism would be gently softened by them saying 'Great men can't be judged like the rest of us' and 'Whatever his faults – and they were many – we must agree that he took the Soviet Union from being a backward peasant society into the nuclear age. The Russians should be more grateful to him and not insult his memory.' It was obvious that behind all this lay an unwillingness to criticise a native son of Georgia who had risen from poverty to rule a fair bit of the world. Any criticism of him was particularly unwelcome from the Russians, Georgia's current villains.

The road between Tbilisi and Gori was in good shape so we arrived without any nail biting after a two hours journey. As we drove into the main square, there he was, the man himself, or at least an enormous statue of him standing in commanding pose surveying the traffic and Gori's present-day citizens.

'They obviously still love him around here,' said Mitch surveying the statue. 'He could hardly be more "in your face" than that.'

We parked in the square. Lado said he had seen it all before, and would go and buy the vodka for the evening supra. The rest of us headed across the square following Tamuna in the direction of a building that looked like a Greek temple and another much larger behind it that looked like a Venetian bank.

'This building,' said Nana pointing to the 'temple', 'is where Stalin was born. The one behind is the museum to his memory.'

'I thought,' said Frank, 'that he was the son of a poor cobbler. How come he was born in a mansion?'

'When we get nearer,' said Nana, 'you will see that this first building – the mansion as you call it – is built around the small wooden house where he was born,' she paused and then continued '… to enshrine it!'

How right she was about the shrine! The 'temple' or 'mansion'did indeed cover a two-roomed wooden building, one room of which had been rented by cobbler Djugashvili and his new wife, and there Joseph was born in 1878. The furniture inside was sparse – a table, chair and stool, a cupboard, a chest of drawers with a copper samovar on top, and an uncomfortable looking bed – all original and all bequests from Stalin's mother. The only dash of colour in the drab scene was a painted chest. Below the room was a cellar, accessed from the street, where Stalin's father plied his trade.

The Greek-style 'temple' enshrining Stalin's birthplace in Gori

'Young Joseph certainly went up in the world,' said Mitch as we made our way to the museum. 'Pity somebody hadn't strangled him at birth. Wouldn't the world have been a better place! Weren't he and his henchmen responsible for the deaths of over 60 million people, and they don't know the full tally yet?'

'I think they might still shoot you for saying things like that in these parts,' Frank said. 'I am sure we all need to be careful what we say about him.'

'When was all this built?' I asked Eka, trying to change the subject. 'In 1957,' she said.

'So that was after Kruschev had denounced Stalin,' I mused.

'Which just proves that we Georgians won't be told what to think by anyone!' said Eka crossly. 'The sooner the Russians realise that, the better.'

Inside the vast museum building, the atmosphere was like a gloomy, dank church that hadn't been used for a while. When we had paid – and then survived the plumbing in the gents – our guide appeared, an ample figure of a woman with the intense, grave expression of one who is about to show you round the tomb of a saint. We followed her up the red carpeted stairs to a half landing where stood another full-size statue of Stalin, this time looking like a rather dashing cavalry officer. Above and behind him was a stained glass window mainly in sombre blue and red which added to the church-like atmosphere. We followed our guide into a large airless room, and there she began her eulogy.

Photographs from the Stalin Museum Gori:
Left. Propaganda picture of a Collective Farm tractor driver
Right. Stalin and his mother, Keke

'Some Mistakes were made…!'

'What a wonderful son the young Stalin had always been to his poor mother, the life-threatening illness and accidents he had survived as a boy, how brilliant he had been at his church school here in Gori and later at the Orthodox seminary in Tbilisi, what a talented poet (and here she pointed to some of his poetic works displayed on the wall), what a brilliant revolutionary fighter, how he had suffered for his beliefs, his spells of exile in Siberia, the role he played in the Bolshevik Revolution, his Five Year Plans, his vision for Soviet industry and agriculture….'

At that point, Mitch could take no more!

'But,' he spluttered as the guide was drawing our attention to photographs of buxom smiling Soviet maidens driving tractors on collective farms, 'but surely he was responsible for the murder of millions of people in the Soviet Union – kulak farmers who resisted collectivisation, poets, priests, authors, generals, admirals, anyone who resisted his insane plans; men, women, children butchered, whole populations and groups starved to death; whole families wiped out, and here too in Georgia his crimes….' he tailed off glaring at our guide as though he held her personally responsible for Stalin and all his works.

'And he was the most dreadful atheist,' Frank added, not to be outdone. 'Surely you Georgians can't admire that side of him with your new found religious zeal.'

The guide's response was magnificently disingenuous! Looking us straight in the eye, she said, 'Yes, some mistakes were made at that time, but we must ask ourselves if Stalin actually knew about the detail of what was happening. He had so much on his mind.'

'Atheist?' she said turning to Frank. 'As a good Communist he had officially to be an atheist but it has now come to light that he always kept a holy Icon in his bedroom, and his valet tells us he prayed to it every night. So perhaps he never really lost his faith, and his mother certainly was a very devout woman and prayed for him constantly.'

'Isn't self-delusion one of the most powerful and dangerous

weapons known to man,' muttered Mitch who, to try to contain himself, had retreated behind a large glass case where presents sent to Stalin on his various birthdays were displayed.

We staggered on past other cases containing Stalin's pipes, cigarette boxes, his military great coat, boots and cap to a display of family photographs including pictures of his two wives – the fact that he had driven them to suicide not mentioned – the son he had left to die at the hands of the Nazis, and his daughter Svetlana whose main claim to fame was that she had survived him, and subsequently fled to live in the USA. But the worst was yet to come! At the end of the long hall, we turned sharp right into what had the feel of a circular tomb. The area was in total darkness except for a single shaft of light which fell on a lily white face in the centre of the room. It was him! Or at any rate his death mask, which seemed to float above a blood-red drape and was so life-like you had the terrifying feeling that at any moment he might open his eyes. We processed clockwise round this thing, and it sent a shiver through all of us. As we reached the exit to this dark gruesome chamber, the guide said, 'please mind the step' but too late! Poor Frank fell forward twisting his ankle.

Stalin's death mask

'He must have heard you calling him an atheist' said Mitch unsympathetically, as Frank hobbled out into the sunshine. 'As a fellow Christian, he wanted revenge!'

'Some Christian!' said Frank. 'How could you let that possibility even cross your mind!

Stalin's armour-plated railway carriage

'Even Dictators have to Go!'

'And now,' said the guide, 'our tour concludes with a visit to the railway carriage used by Stalin on his tours throughout the Soviet Union. It is also the carriage he used when he travelled to meet Prime Minister Churchill and President Roosevelt at the Yalta Conference in 1945.'

Earlier we had paused by a long green railway carriage on our way into the museum, and Frank, who for some reason knew about such things, had remarked on how heavily armour plated it was, but we had been hurried past it by Tamuna. Our guide now led us round the side of the museum to where the railway carriage stood, and unlocked the door. We were ushered inside and along a narrow communicating corridor running off which were several large compartments.

'This was the room for Stalin's bodyguards,' said the guide, opening the door of the first compartment, 'and this was the kitchen,' she continued opening the adjoining compartment door. Next came the radio room, then Stalin's bedroom. This was much more spacious so we went in to look around. Here was his bed, wardrobe, dressing table, chair, other everyday items one of the most ruthless men who ever lived had touched and used, all so immediate and so intimate that you almost felt he had just left the room for a moment. But we were about to get even more up front and personal with Stalin.

Stalin's desk & toilet in his private railway carriage.
Stalin Museum Gori

'What's through here?' I said, pointing to a door leading off the bedroom.

'That is his bathroom and lavatory,' said the guide.

'Don't be surprised if he is still in there!' said Mitch, and our laughter broke the tension.

Frank opened the door and we crowded in. Here was his bath, wash hand basin and, yes, his lavatory!

'One of his many thrones,' muttered Mitch, and in best American fashion aiming his camera at the loo!

'Whoever made that remark about the banality of evil should see this,' said Frank looking around the tiny room. 'This gives it a whole new dimension!'

Out in the corridor again, we moved on to the largest compartment of all which doubled as a sitting and dining room. Frank sat down at the desk that occupied one corner.

'Only God knows how many infamous decrees were penned and death warrants signed here,' he murmured.

'That's when he even took time to bother keeping up with the paperwork,' said Mitch.

And in best tourist fashion, we all took turns at being photographed sitting on the various chairs in various disrespectful poses while the guide looked on disapprovingly.

Then out into the sunlight and the fresh air, and never was escape from anywhere so welcome. It had been fascinating to see the carriage – more interesting by far than the sanitised museum in that it was a real brush with history, however unnerving that encounter had been. But I think we had all a sense of having crossed the path of something monstrous, had caught a glimpse of its scaly tail before it disappeared, and we knew that the evil that fuelled it was still with us, in every sense of the word, in our world too. As we emerged from the gloom of the carriage, we were greeted with the cheery sight of a group of young children playing around in the sunshine while their teacher bought the tickets for the museum.

'I hope they are not subjected to all that blatant propaganda,' mused Frank.

'Care to bet?' said Mitch.

'Uncle Joe's Vodka'

'How did you enjoy your encounter with our Mr Stalin?' asked Tamuna and, perhaps warned off by our looks of uncertainty about what to say, she continued quickly, ' of course, we all now know the dreadful things for which he was responsible, and our view of him has changed greatly in recent years.'

'Why then,' asked Frank with uncharacteristic force, 'was all this built after he had been denounced by Khruschev, and his dreadful crimes had been made known to the whole world? Why is there nothing in these....' he paused to get the right word, '...these "shrines" ... about his purges and the plain fact that he was a mass murderer?'

Tamuna adopted her school mistress look. 'You must understand,' she said, 'that these "shrines" as you call them were Beria's idea....and anyway,' she continued, 'surely you agree that the reputation of leaders can change when different historical perspectives are brought to bear on their actions, and new facts about them come to light.'

With that, and with us now firmly put in our place, we made our way back to Lado and the car where he proudly displayed his purchases of the morning.

'I don't believe this,' Mitch could hardly contain himself again. The vodka was labelled 'Stalin Vodka' above a picture of the man himself looking like anyone's fond uncle. We bit our tongues for friendship's sake and were soon on our way to the beautiful town of Borjomi to sample its spa waters.

'You have not shaken Stalin off just yet,' said Tamuna. 'Up in Borjomi you may get to sleep in his bed!'

Summer Palaces, Spa Water and Dead Cabbage

The drive up the valley of the river Mtkvari from Gori to Borjomi is delightful. The river makes its exuberant way from the 'Lesser Caucasus' which separate Georgia from Turkey through Tbilisi to the Caspian, and is clearly in a great hurry. It sparkles and clatters its way through Borjomi and this, together with the high hills of the great National Park that wrap themselves around the town, helps to make Borjomi a gem of a place.

It was a favourite retreat of the great, if not particularly good, in the nineteenth century, when its star status was crowned by a palace built by Duke Mikhail Romanov, son of the Russian Tsar Nicholas I. The Duke's son suffered from asthma, and the mountain air and spa water found in Borjomi brought him some relief. The Romanov hangers-on soon arrived too, building lovely balconied houses on the valley sides.

Come the Bolshevik revolution, Stalin arrived, and used the Duke's palace as a summer retreat thus transforming it into yet another shrine to Georgia's native son. Our meetings were to be held in the Romanov Palace grounds which also contained a

One of the summer villas in Borjomi built for Russian aristocrats

sanatorium, so favoured by the Soviet rulers as a 'treat' for the workers, and where they could, like the aristocrats of old, take the waters, have mud baths and generally 'chill out'.

We were housed in a large wooden chalet and, when we had settled in, Tamuna went off to see if we could have a tour around the Duke's Palace.

'And then you can lie in Stalin's bed,' she said continuing to tease us. 'I can see all three of you are now so much in love with him! In the meantime,' continued Tamuna, 'you must all try the spa water; it will do you so much good.'

Frank, who was always seeking purification of some sort or other, tried the water first when we arrived at the elaborate spa well overlooking the river. We watched him as his face turned greenish-grey at the first sip!

'That is repulsive,' he gasped, handing the metal container to Mitch. 'Ah, you religious guys can't take your medicine,' said Mitch helping himself to a large gulp, and then immediately spitting it out all over my feet.

'My God,' he said. 'I'll sue them. That's revolting!'

Now it was my turn. It smelt like sulphur and indeed tasted vile. I had been expecting the spa-water to taste something like the Borjomi mineral water which we had always found so palatable but apparently spa-water is only a very distant relative of the mineral variety. When we had recovered ourselves, we strolled back for the evening meal in the sanatorium's restaurant. Frank cast a baleful eye over our fellow diners, of whom there must have been several hundred.

'Do you think they all looked as old and ill before they started their water treatment or has the spa water done that to them?' he pondered.

'Or the food?' said Mitch, looking at the mess of dead vegetable matter and wizened up meat balls that had just arrived on our table.

'I think the food here is designed to be somewhat unappetising,' Tamuna said across the table, 'after all, these people are here for the good of their health and to purge themselves, so appetising food is not important. Indeed, to get best results from their stay, they must not be encouraged to eat much.'

'Well, the kitchen folk can rest easy,' said Mitch, 'they sure are doing a great job.'

'But I think we should be eating rather better,' Tamuna reflected pushing something over-cooked and purple-coloured, which may have once been cabbage, round her plate. 'I will contact one of the local restaurants to send us in a nice supra.'

'Can you actually get a carry-out supra?' I was prompted to ask.

'Oh yes indeed,' said Tamuna, 'I will simply specify what we all want. We already have Lado's vodka, and of course lots of Borjomi good mineral water. Not the spa water' she added reassuringly. 'So we will not need wine this evening.'

That evening the supra took the usual form, with lots of Georgia's delicious food, washed down with Borjomi's mineral water and Georgian vodka which, I was told by Mitch, who claimed he was a connoisseur, was also 'darn good stuff' even if the label on the bottle had the face of a heartless dictator emblazoned on it.

'And so to Bed…'

'If they insist we lie in Stalin's bed, even for a gag, I may need a shot of something strong myself,' said Frank. 'You don't think Tamuna and the others are serious, do you?'

But our delightful Georgian friends were serious! Next morning, far too early considering the delicate state of our stomachs, Tamuna arrived at breakfast flushed with success. It appeared she had had a difficult time persuading the security guards at the Palace to let us in because Georgia's President now uses it as a summer home, and the guards were hourly expecting him and his family to arrive on the nearby helipad to begin a short stay. But somehow Tamuna had managed to get us in so long as we took no photographs, carried no baggage, and didn't stay long.

'This is the second time you have fallen under suspicion of trying to assassinate their President,' said Mitch 'You Irish have a lot to live down.'

At the Palace entrance we were greeted by a guide who bore a remarkable resemblance to Corporal Jones in 'Dad's Army'.

The Russian Summer Palace

He immediately tried to sell us postcards, and once we had succumbed to his marketing skills, he led the way through the house. It was, of course, sumptuously furnished, and had the most magnificent views across the river to the steep hills which rose abruptly on the other bank, and on which were perched the ruins of a turreted medieval castle and an ancient church.

'These aristocrats could sure pick the best spots,' said Frank.

Eventually we arrived back in the hallway where we had first entered. 'Where is it?' asked Mitch. 'Did we walk past it?'

We all knew what he meant – that bed! – and curiosity had now got the better of all of us. For some unfathomable reason, we now didn't want to leave without seeing it.

'Stalin used the palace as a summer home,' I ventured, 'did he stay here often?'

'Marshal Stalin was here on only two occasions that we know of, one in the 1920s and then near the end of his life in the early 1950s,' said 'Corporal Jones'.

'And is there anything to see associated with Stalin,' I persisted, 'we have visited his home and museum in Gori....' I was getting desperate.

'Oh you want to see the famous bed,' said our guide, who we now suspected of teasing us too. 'Yes, since you are so interested in our history, I will show you of course.'

He took us into a room close to the entrance porch and so surprisingly located on the ground floor, and there it was!

'Well a bed is a bed is a bed,' said Mitch sitting down on it.

'I wouldn't sit there for any money,' said Frank, as I too made my way across the room towards it. 'You never know what you would catch.'

'Don't Panic, Corporal Jones!'

I was just about to join Mitch on the end of the bed when 'Corporal Jones', who seemed taken by surprise by Mitch and my histrionics, became very flustered and stopped me in mid stride.

'Please,' he said, 'I ask you to be respectful. Do not sit on the bed, and no photographs!' as Mitch added insult to injury by producing his camera.

'They sure take their shrines – ancient and modern – very seriously,' said Mitch as 'Corporal Jones' propelled us towards the door.

'Of course,' 'Corporal Jones' said, sensing another selling opportunity, '....if you want to buy some more postcards, perhaps I could permit....' But the moment had passed.

'I've had enough of Stalin to last me a lifetime,' declared Mitch.

'And anyway,' said the ever wary Frank, 'it could have been anybody's bed! Who's to know! Just as who's to know if Stalin kept that icon in his room in the Kremlin. But icon or no icon, he certainly wasn't a good and a God-fearing man.'

'Maybe that because he thought he was God,' said Mitch dryly.

Chapter 10

Cave Cities & Silk Roads

Vardzia Cave City

'Oil!' said Pete emphatically, 'That's all the West is interested in here in Georgia. Take that new oil pipe line they have built from the Caspian right across Georgia to the Black Sea. Well, that says it all! And that's why the Yanks are pouring money in here. Did you know that Georgia gets the third biggest grant from the US per head of population after Israel and Egypt? Oil is the new silk!'

'New what?' said Frank looking puzzled.

'Silk,' repeated Pete. 'Surely you know that the old Silk Road linking Europe to China went right through the heart of Georgia!'

'Of course I knew that,' said Frank, now on the defensive,

'though I think it wasn't the main Silk Road,' he added, trying to put Pete off his stride.

'Well,' Pete continued, oblivious, as ever, of the offence his high-handed tone was causing, 'I have read that Marco Polo travelled through here on his way from Venice to China, and God knows how many others over the centuries. But now its oil, the new black silk.'

Pete was an ambitious young salesman whose firm had sent him out to report back to them in London on contract possibilities in Georgia. He seemed to have come to the conclusion early on that Georgia was already sewn up – or 'stitched up' as he kept saying – by the Yanks, an attitude which made for strained relationships between himself and Frank and Mitch. Pete was from the North of England and had none of the polish or reserve of his southern fellow-country men, added to which he seemed to take a perverse delight in annoying my two American friends on every possible occasion. Since we all lived in the same hotel, his opportunities for irritating them were many and various. Mitch had taken one of his instant dislikes to Pete, and delighted in giving as good as he got. Poor Frank tried to do his Christian duty and not retaliate, but was not always successful.

Pete had done his homework on Georgia, past and present, and was always eager to give us a history, geography or economics lesson which was invariably delivered in his combative style.

'Arrogant English asshole!' Mitch would mutter darkly. 'Now I know why you Irish have had so many problems with the English over the centuries!'

But truth to tell I got on well with Pete for he was a fund of interesting and often useful information about Georgia. He also had one major attribute in my eyes and one endearing weakness. He had hired a four wheel drive which, unlike the Georgians, he drove carefully, and he generously took us with him in his jeep across the length and breadth of the country on days off. His endearing weakness was his passion for beautiful Georgian women, and these he also took with him across the length and breadth of Georgia!

'I wouldn't mind,' said Frank, 'but it's a new one every time! And such lovely women! Where does he get them? And why does he take us with him on his dates? Of course, I am very glad he does. We have seen parts of Georgia we would never have got to otherwise, but it's very odd. You must admit, he is a very strange guy.'

'It's obvious why he takes you with him, Frank,' said Mitch. 'It's to keep him on the straight and narrow. He takes the rest of us as his audience. He's a dude who always needs an audience, and the Georgian women, however beautiful, are no use to him when he is giving one of his 'sermons'. As for where he gets these dames, look around you! Young Georgian women are very beautiful, or is even looking at them against your religion, Frank? And I'll tell you why it is a different dame every time! These Georgian beauties are no fools. They soon discover what an arrogant asshole he is, and ditch him pretty darn quick. And who could blame them!'

'You will want to come with me to see Mtskheta, the old capital?" Pete issued this invitation like an ultimatum over breakfast one Saturday morning. I had wanted to visit Mtskheta ever since Andreo and I had skirted it on our way to the Georgian Military Highway so I volunteered immediately. Since it was only about an hour's drive from Tbilisi, Mitch and Frank obviously thought they could just about stand Pete for that length of time so they signed up to go too. Pete disappeared after breakfast and reappeared half an hour later with one of his lovely girlfriends. She was called Irma, and was introduced to us as someone who knew about the history of Mtskheta and the fabulous Cave City nearby called Uplistsikhe, which we could also take in on this trip.

'Irma speaks very good English,' said Pete.

'Let's hope she gets using it with him around,' muttered Mitch.

'I think we should first go to Jvari Church up there on the mountain,' said Irma as we approached the outskirts of

Mtskheta, 'from there you will get a magnificent view of the old capital, and Jvari itself is very beautiful and interesting.' Pete drove up the steep road to the church, and even before we got out of the jeep we could see that the views were indeed magnificent. The old city of Mtskheta down below was situated at the confluence of two broad rivers along one of which ran the beginning of the Georgian Military Highway.

Mtskheta; Georgia's old capital

Inside, Jvari Church was candlelit and beautiful, and made all the more so by a baptism ceremony that was going on when we entered.

'You have heard of St. Nino, the slave girl who first brought Christianity to Georgia in the fourth century?' said Irma, and without waiting for an answer she continued, 'it was here on the site of this church that Nino first set up her famous cross, indeed "jvari" means cross in Georgian. St. Nino took her stand here, defying the priests who served the great pagan idols she could see down there in the square in Mtskheta. She triumphed over the pagans, as you know, and so Georgia became one of the first countries in the world to adopt Christianity as its official religion. We are very proud of that, and the memory of St. Nino's triumph has helped us to survive so many disasters, even Soviet atheism in the twentieth century.' Irma then crossed herself several times in the Orthodox fashion as if to exorcise an evil memory.

'To think,' muttered Mitch back in the jeep, 'that this Nino woman did all that without a strategic or operational or action plan or even a job description! If Georgia could only get her back today this place would soon be humming!'

'Nino must have had great faith,' Frank said solemnly. 'She sure had something going for her,' said Mitch.

We dropped down into the town at the heart of which stands the ancient cathedral, proof in stone that St. Nino had won the day over the pagans almost two thousand years ago. As we walked towards the cathedral, trying to avoid the eyes of old women begging and the stall holder trying to sell us replicas of St Nino's cross, Irma told us how the Saint had platted her hair with vine leaves which explained the distinctive shape of her cross. This prompted Frank to say in a serious voice:

'And you Georgians have never managed to disentangle your Christianity from strong drink ever since.' Luckily Irma didn't appear to understand.

St Nino's Cross. The Saint is said to have created the original using her hair and vine leaves

'This cathedral is the ancient spiritual heart of Georgia,' Irma continued after we had crossed a large courtyard and finally reached the entrance. 'Inside you will see the tombs of very many of our Kings and Queens. I think it is like Westminster Abbey in London, very ancient with many royal tombs.'

'Are King David the Builder and Queen Tamara buried here too,' I asked mainly because they were the only two Georgian monarchs I could call to mind.

'No, neither,' said Irma, 'Queen Tamara's grave is unknown. Legend has it that when she died in 1212AD, Svan warriors came down from Svaneti and took her body and wagons laden with her treasures back up there to the High Caucasus to bury her. Then, so that the whereabouts of her grave would never be discovered, the warriors killed each other, the last one falling on his own sword.'

'My memory of the Svans,' said Mitch to me when he thought Irma was out of earshot, 'is that the best way to keep a secret from them is to call a meeting and try to tell them. If our experience up in Svaneti is anything to go by, those warriors had totally the wrong approach!'

Irma suddenly remembered my question about the tomb of King David the Builder and rejoined us to say:

'King David is buried in the monastery he founded at the city of Gelati in the west of Georgia, and where he also established a university. His grave is interesting for he gave instructions that he should be buried in the main gateway to the monastery so that everyone entering would walk over him.'

'What a modest, humble man,' said Frank.

'Or was it just arrogance?' countered Mitch. 'Was he not just making sure he would never be forgotten?'

Irma looked puzzled, and must have concluded that we were disappointed in Mtskheta Cathedral because it did not contain the tombs of the only two Georgian monarchs we had heard about. She led the way up towards the beautiful iconostasis which hides the altar from view in Orthodox churches, and pointed to a stone slab sunk in the floor.

'Here is buried King Vakhtang Gorgasali, Georgia's 'Wolf-Lion' King, who founded Tbilisi in the fifth century, and who moved the capital from here in Meskheta to there.' She looked at us to see if we were now suitably impressed, 'and here is the tomb of King Irakli II who signed the Treaty of Gurgievsk in 1783 placing Georgia under the protection of the Russian Tsars only to be betrayed so cruelly by them. For you know,' she continued with feeling, 'they took advantage of our fear of our Muslim neighbours in Turkey and Persia, violated the treaty, usurped our country and deposed our king. They even imposed their Russian Orthodox style of worship on us, whitewashing over the beautiful wall frescoes that were unique to our ancient Orthodox churches and replacing them with their icons. Georgia was Christian and Orthodox hundreds of years before Russia had even heard of Christianity. They have always been jealous of our history and culture,' she concluded, her eyes suddenly flashing intensely.

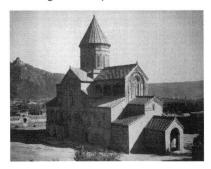 

Mtskheta's eleventh century Cathedral contains the grave of Georgia's 'Lion-King' Vakhtang Gorgasali who moved the capital from Meskheta to Tbilisi

Pete, who had been strangely silent for a while couldn't contain himself any longer and launched into one of what Mitch called his 'sermons'.

'Doesn't that explain a lot about the present day?' he had

adopted his irritating combative tone. 'Russia and Georgia feel betrayed by each other! The Georgians because the Russians annexed their country back then, the Russians because Georgia was one of the first countries to break away and declare independence when the old Soviet system collapsed. That hit Moscow hard. The satellite countries in Eastern Europe – Poland, East Germany, Hungary, all those – they had only been under Russian control since 1945 and so it was no great surprise for them to break with Moscow when the Soviet Union collapsed, but the relations between Georgia and Russia go back much farther. The Russians had got used to the idea that Georgia was genuinely a part of Russia. They holidayed here on the Black Sea and at Georgia's spas, enjoyed Georgia's climate, its food and wine. Did you know that the great majority of good restaurants in Moscow are still Georgian?'

'Well, we do now,' muttered Mitch. 'All that guy needs is a pulpit! Let's leave him here in the cathedral. He's in his element.'

Pete may not have chosen the best moment to lecture us, but he was right. During our stay, we too had all suffered from Russia's wrath in a small way over Georgia's new love affair with the USA, with the EU and, worst red rag of all, by her avowed intention to join NATO. This most recent tug-of-war over Georgia just confirms that it is as important an international crossroads as ever. Here East meets West, Great Powers collide, and promises are made and broken.

Uplistsikhe Cave City

Massacred Monks

The next site we visited that Saturday would have been a place of pure romance had it not also been the site of many massacres. We went on to the great Cave City of Uplistsikhe which, Irma explained, had been a major stopping place on the ancient Silk Road. We could see the remains of the city from a distance, and even Mitch seemed excited by the sight. Tier upon tier of caves and tunnels cut into the cream coloured rock were exposed to view across a large expanse of mountainside. As we approached it, with the afternoon sun beating down, the site looked like a gigantic honeycomb set on its side. Once we had paid the small admission fee, a guide called Zura led us up a very steep path to what he called Uplistsikhe's Main Street.

'This site has been inhabited for almost three thousand years,' he explained, 'and in its hey-day over twenty thousand people lived here.'

He pointed out stone stalls to right and left of the 'street' where merchants of all kinds had plied their trade over the centuries. There was a chemist shop where all kind of herbs and potions had been found, a prison sunk deep in the ground which must have been a fearsome place in which to be incarcerated, next to it wine and grain cellars, a pagan temple with an ominous looking basin for performing sacrifices of all kinds, then a theatre with a recognisable orchestra pit, a palace associated with Queen Tamara and, high up on the top of the site, a church, for in its later days Uplistiskhe was inhabited by 5000 monks. Zura seemed particularly proud of his Georgian ancestors' skill at getting water to the site, and explained this to us in detail, showing us the elaborate ceramic pipe system that had brought water from almost five miles away high up on the mountain.

'These people obviously lived their lives vertically,' said Mitch. 'The trouble they took to make places like this habitable! It's like the cave cities of the Anasazi Peoples of the Mesa Verde back home in Colorado. It remains a mystery why the people who lived in the Mesa Verde ever deserted the site? Do they know why, after so long and so much effort to make the place comfortable, this site was deserted?'

'It is not a mystery here at Uplistsikhe,' said Zura, 'The answer is Genghis Khan and the Mongols. They swept through Georgia at the end of Queen Tamara's golden reign, killing her successor and massacring all before them. They massacred every living thing here at Uplistsikhe including the 5000 monks. The site was never reinhabited and the ravages of time and earthquakes have done the rest.'

We looked down into the river far below, and could now see

exactly what Zura meant.

'Isn't it strange,' mused Frank as we clamoured back down the stony steep pathway from the city, 'how much all these people know about their culture and history, and how alive it is for them. To hear this guy, you would think Genghis Khan had come through yesterday.'

Again Pete took upon himself to explain, 'The education system in the old Soviet Union was very good,' he said. 'There was none of this modern "find out for yourself" stuff you find in the West. They were told to learn it off and get on with it.'

Whatever the reason, Frank certainly had a point. The knowledge of the average Georgian was often remarkable. Everybody seemed to speak two or three languages well; their knowledge of their history, literature and indeed world literature was formidable. I had an animated discussion about Oscar Wilde's plays with a Tbilisi taxi driver when he heard I was from Ireland. It was not unusual to find Georgians who were familiar with the work of Dickens, the Brontes, Galsworthy and many others.

Mitch had his own explanation:
'In Soviet times, it paid to keep your head down, and the simplest and best place to keep it was stuck in a book. That's why they are all so well read. Still, you're right, Frank; its impressive just the same,' he concluded, studiously ignoring Pete's thoughts on the subject.

There are two other Cave Cities in Georgia, one called Davit-Gareja in the east of the country, right on the border with Azerbaijan, and the other to the south called Vardzia near the Turkish border. In many ways these are more spectacular if infinitely less accessible than Uplistsikhe. I accompanied Pete to both, each time with a different girlfriend. The function of these, and indeed their fate, was very similar to that of Uplistsikhe. They guarded both the Silk Road and the borders of Georgia over the centuries, and their history was similarly and sadly also bathed in blood.

Davit-Gareja Cave City

Miserable Monks

Davit-Gareja was undoubtedly the most sacred of Georgia's Cave Cities having been a monastery for most of its existence, as it is again today.

'You must be careful not to offend the monks,' Pete's latest girlfriend, Sopho, warned us as we trundled along the appallingly

The monks cave cells at Davit-Gareja Cave City

badly surfaced road through Georgia's eastern semi-desert to get to the site. 'They are very strict Orthodox, and they do not welcome men with cameras, women in short skirts, or noise of any kind. Davit-Gareja contains the sixth century tomb of St. David which they tend with great devotion.'

Sopho's warning was timely. Davit-Gareja was the only place in Georgia where I felt I was not wanted. The site of the monastery's churches and caves was spectacular, but the monk who took us around was more like a prison warder than a guide. His mood may not have been helped by the group of Americans also visiting who clearly had not been warned about short dresses, cameras or noise.

'Are you from Ireland?' screamed an ample lady over the altar-like tomb of St David. 'You and I have something in common. My birthday is the March 17, St Patrick's Day.'

The sixth century tomb of St David in the Rock Church,
Davit-Gareja Cave City

'I'm glad that's all you and she have in common,' said Pete rather too loudly for comfort.

Pete declared that he had read somewhere that some of the monks at Davit-Gareja were, in fact, exiled there for their opposition to the American presence in Georgia.

'It seems that US Christian churches of various kinds, and with bags of money, have arrived in Georgia on the back of the American aid, and this has made some of the Georgian Orthodox clerics go ballistic,' Pete explained. 'These Yankee churches will offer Georgians anything – well- equipped free schools for their children here in Georgia, subsidized university places back in the US – if they will switch their religious allegiance to them. It must be a big temptation if you are a civil servant or a teacher say, on a small salary or no salary at all, and you want the best for your kids. Anyway, this article I read said that the Orthodox Church here is understandably furious. They have survived two thousand years of never ending invasions and persecutions, and then sixty years of militant Communist atheism, so they are not going to allow themselves to be side-lined now by a bunch of happy-clappy holy rollers from the US with money to bribe people. It seems some Orthodox monks have spoken out claiming that the Georgian Church, and indeed Georgia too, would be better off cosying up to the Russians again for at least the 'Ruskies' are their fellow Orthodox. The Tbilisi government don't like this kind of talk for, as you know, they are busy wooing the US, so the article in the paper said they stepped in to get some of the more outspoken monks exiled here. Maybe that's why these blokes look so hostile.' he concluded, casting a glance at our 'warder'.

Sopho, who had been listening intently, said thoughtfully, 'You surely understand that for centuries the existence of the Georgian Church has been threatened and has had to protect itself. It was here at Davit-Gareja that 6000 monks were slaughtered during the Easter Night Procession by the army of the Muslim Persian Shah in 1615. And,' here she paused to emphasise her next point 'would you believe that in Soviet times, in the twentieth century, this important two thousand year old monastic site was used by the Russian army for target practice! It is a miracle that any of it survives! It is a miracle that the Georgian Church has survived!'

'To understand all is to forgive all,' said Pete. 'Maybe these Orthodox guys have a lot to be up-tight about!' and taking Sopho by the hand he continued, 'Let's leave these moody monks to it, and see if we can get some dinner.'

Unfortunately he was out of luck; dinner was a good two hours away back along the cratered road we had come, but we had the consolation that when we sat down to eat the usual glorious Georgian meal, it was accompanied by the best wines in Georgia for we were in the Kakheti region, where the very best grapes produce the very best Georgian wines.

'We must tackle Frank tomorrow about what his fundament-alist church friends are up to here in Georgia,' said Pete sleepily after dinner. But we never did!

The Intoxicating Tears of Queen Tamara

Vardzia Cave City

'I think this is may be the one,' said Pete as I set out on yet another expedition with him, this time to Georgia's third Cave City, Vardzia. 'She is called Mariami, and she really is a dish, and smart too.'

Mariami was indeed stunningly beautiful, also great company on the journey and, like so many Georgians, very knowledgeable about her country so a fund of information about all we were to see on the way to Vardzia, and about the Cave City itself when we got there. Vardzia is very near Georgia's frontier with Turkey, and the road to the site was as spectacular as it was cratered. We followed the valley of the river Mtkvari from its fertile lower reaches up through mountain passes which, though not as dramatic as those in the High Caucasus on the Georgian Military Highway in the north, were still magnificent. Instead of snow they were blanketed with the richest shade of green sward worthy of Ireland's 'forty shades' at their best.

On the road to Vardzia

We arrived at Vardzia at noon and, under a sweltering sun, made our way as quickly as possible up the steep path to shelter in the shade of the city's bell tower. There we were met by Lacha, who was to guide us through the labyrinth of cave dwellings and churches.

'This is the most famous, and I think the most spectacular, of Georgia's Cave Cities,' said Mariami, 'because of its connection with Queen Tamara. You will see her fresco in the Church of the Assumption here in the heart of the city. It was painted in the twelfth century in her lifetime and so must be a good likeness. The city is on 19 levels on the cliff face but you must only climb as high as you wish. The higher levels can be frightening.'

Vardzia Cave City

Lacha led us along a path which ran the length of the lowest level but still had a terrifying sheer drop to our right. We passed rooms that had once been soldiers' barracks, monks' cells, wine presses, bakeries, stores, and elaborate living quarters until we arrived at the church at the centre of the rock face. There we were greeted by a friendly young monk who invited us in and pointed to the frescos which we were assured were untouched since the church was consecrated in the twelfth century.

'So that's what Queen Tamara actually looked like,' said Pete to Mariami, 'I think you are much more beautiful.'

Mariami ignored this bit of clumsy flattery and said, 'It

Detail from the fresco of Georgia's twelfth century monarch Queen Tamara in the Church at Vardzia Cave City

must be unusual to have a picture of a twelfth century queen painted when she was alive. You could almost imagine she is still here in Vardzia. Her presence makes this a mystical place for us Georgians. Here we can feel like a nation again in the presence of our most successful monarch who presided over Georgia's Golden Age. Here we can feel the true importance of our Church, for Queen Tamara required the 2000 monks living here in her time to pray daily for Georgia's prosperity and safety. Vardzia has a very special meaning for me and my friends because, in Soviet times, the Russians put it out of bounds and only the army was allowed in this region because it is so close to the NATO bases in Turkey. But now Georgia has shaken off all that, and all Georgians can come here when they like! I am so happy to be here again,' and there were tears in her eyes.

'And finally,' said Lacha, as we left the monk to his devotions in the church, 'come and see the "Tears of Queen Tamara".' He lit tapers, and led the way along a dark passage to a wooden ladder leading steeply down into an echoing chamber in the very heart of the mountain. There he lit more tapers and handed a bundle to each of us.

'Here are the tears of Queen Tamara,' he said pointing to the centre of the cavern.

Even in the uncertain light we could see a crystal clear deep pool shimmering in front of us. It sparkled in the most magical way. Lacha produced a tin mug, dipped it in the pool and handed it to me. The water tasted ice cold and sweet. The others took a sip too.

'For some reason it feels intoxicating,' said Pete thoughtfully. And for some reason which we were at a loss to explain, it did.

'I suppose the water has trickled down through those rocks for millions of years,' said Pete. But we knew that did not explain its spell.

We bade Lacha farewell and started on the long journey back to Tbilisi. Georgia, that land of never-ending surprises, had just produced another in the form of a Queen's intoxicating tears.

The Land where Legends come to Life

'Well I don't know where the beautiful Mariami has disappeared to or why it didn't work out, but she is not coming with Pete to Vani,' I said in response to questions from my two American friends.

'Good,' said Frank, 'I can sleep easy knowing there is nothing going on.'

Something 'going on' between Pete and his many girlfriends bothered Frank to the point of obsession.

'Those fundamentalist Christians are all the same,' said Mitch when I mentioned Frank's pre-occupation. 'They are all sex mad. Well, face it, if you don't drink, smoke, gamble, or sin generally what's left for them to think about except sex and religion? So Pete is not having any company with him on this trip except us,' he continued, 'that's a pity. Those lovely women he pulls are the only thing makes him half bearable.'

But I had underestimated Pete! He vanished briefly in the jeep as he always did before one of our weekend expeditions and returned shortly afterwards with yet another beautiful Georgian girlfriend, this time called Mzia. When we asked why we had not been introduced to her until now, Pete said he had been keeping her 'out of sight' she was so precious to him. Mitch looked daggers and Frank gave a series of his well-rehearsed disapproving sniffs. Pete, his macho image again in the ascendant, looked triumphant.

Having put us all in the shade, he was, as always, generous with the four-wheel drive, and this weekend had invited us to come with him to western Georgia to visit the archaeological site at Vani. It was said to have been the capital of Colchis, the ancient name for Georgia, and so was assumed to be where the legendary Jason and his Argonauts had come to find the Golden Fleece. It was also said to be where Jason met the sorceress Medea and her father King Aetes who had set him the impossible tasks to win the Fleece.

'I knew two of the guys who sailed with Tim Severin when he reconstructed Jason's ship, and set off to prove that it was no fairytale, and that it had all happened,' Pete was in full flow. 'Have you read Severin's book?' he demanded clearly hoping we hadn't, 'tough journey, tough men, but they proved the journey was possible.'

'I read somewhere,' Frank had decided not to be outdone, 'that the Golden Fleece may actually have existed. Apparently until quite recently it was normal practice in the High Caucasus to put sheep fleeces across the rivers in spring to catch particles of gold being brought down in the melt water from the mountain snow. Some of these fleeces trapped so many nuggets they looked as if they were made of pure gold.'

'Well however the folk of Colchis got it,' said Pete who never liked to be told anything, 'we know there was plenty of gold around in those days. Have you seen the exhibition of Colchis' gold in the National Museum in Tbilisi?'

We all hastened to assure him that we had seen that magnificent exhibition to forestall him preaching one of his sermons about it.

The journey to Vani took several hours but we arrived in time to visit the museum near the excavation site. We were shown round the exhibits by a guide who was also working on the 'dig' so his knowledge of the period and the artefacts was all-encompassing. Gold jewellery made by the finest craftsmen had been buried with the nobility of Colchis in the seventh and sixth Centuries BC and were steadily coming to light as the tombs at Vani were uncovered. These treasures, together with magnificent ceramics and bronze statues from later periods, were beautifully displayed. Towards the end of our tour of the museum, we detected that our guide was getting a bit impatient if we lingered too long over some of the superb finds.

Mzia explained.

'This is Georgia's National Day and the museum staff are having a supra. Our guide does not want to miss it, and has invited us to come too.'

'Oh no,' said Frank, and for once we all agreed and did our best to think of convincing excuses.

'Does that mean we can't visit the actual archaeological site?' asked Pete.

We could see the site on the other side of the road, and that it was linked to the museum by a footbridge with a locked gate. Mzia came to the rescue again. After a brief conversation with the guide, he handed her the key to the footbridge.

'We are to post the key through the letter box of the museum when we have visited the site,' she explained. So nothing, not even Jason and his Fleece, was allowed to come between a Georgian and his supra.

'These people have their priorities right,' said Mitch as we made our way across the bridge.

The actual Vani site was rather like Navan Fort back in Northern Ireland in that you had to use your imagination to conjure up the vibrant, wealthy city of antiquity and the citizens who had once lived there, not to speak of Jason, Medea, King Aetes and the others in the legend. Here and there were signs of the on-going excavations, and the place was strewn with ancient roof tiles and similar objects. Picking up one of these that looked like a piece of everyday pottery, Frank said:

'It's objects like these that make this place more understandable to me than the jewellery, magnificent as that is. It helps you to get a glimpse of ordinary folk doing ordinary thing all those centuries ago.'

With the sun setting over Vani, we made our way back across the footbridge, deposited the key as instructed and got back in the jeep. It was too late and too far to think about returning to Tbilisi that night so we would have to find somewhere to stay. Pete consulted his guide book.

Walking on Kings

'What do you know about King David the Builder?' he asked in his best schoolmaster fashion.

Frank volunteered an answer 'Isn't he the guy your friend Irma told us about when she was showing us around the cathedral in Mtskheta? Wasn't he the king who wanted everyone to walk all over his grave?'

I thought the emphasis Frank had placed on 'your friend Irma' spoke volumes in terms of his disapproval of Pete's 'Romeo' tendencies, but Pete wisely ignored it.

'Right,' he said with not a hint of embarrassment, 'we are actually quite close to where he is buried. Let's go and walk on him tomorrow.'

King David the Builder lies in the monastic site he himself built in the twelfth century at Gelati which is indeed close to Vani and was our destination the next morning. It turned out to be a real treasure which we might easily have missed. We arrived just as a ferocious thunderstorm broke overhead and this, combined with the service going on as we entered the 'Cathedral of the Virgin' near the present day entrance to the monastery, created a definite Doomsday effect. The twelfth century frescoes in the church, of which one of the most striking is that of King David himself, were painted in fantastically vivid colours while over the apse was one of Georgia's greatest works of art, an enormous mosaic composed of over two million pieces.

King David the Builder's twelfth century cathedral, monastic site and university at Gelati

The gold vestments and crowns of the priests before the sparkling iconostasis, the chanting of the choir, the light from dozens of candles, the heavy scent of incense, the vast glowing mosaic in the apse, the dazzling frescoes all around the walls, and the storm raging outside combined to create a scene of high drama. We were all affected. Then Pete broke the spell, and literally brought me back down to earth.

'Watch out for Frank,' he whispered, 'he'll think The End has come!'

The storm soon passed and outside beyond the Cathedral we made our way to the ruins of the twelfth century university also built by King David.

'He built it to bring Neo-Platonist philosophy to Georgia,' explained Mzia.

'For heaven's sake don't ask what that is,' said Mitch, 'or friend Pete will keep us here all day!'

If Pete knew anything about the Neo-Platonists he kept it to himself. Instead he sprinted across to the far side of the ruins to stand on a stone podium where his guide book said the professors had stood when lecturing their students a thousand years ago. There he insisted on having several photographs taken while he adopting the pose of a stern medieval lecturer.

'What a loss he has been to the Neo-Platonists!' said Mitch dryly. 'Now where is this guy's grave that we came here to walk all over?'

1. King David the Builder's Grave. Ancient entrance gate to Gelati Monastic complex

2. Portrait of King David the Builder in the Cathedral of the Virgin, monastic complex Gelati

When we found King David's grave in the ancient south gateway to the monastery, it was covered with an enormous well-worn slab on which some admirer had placed a bunch of white lilies. As requested by the great man way back in the twelfth century, we duly walked all over him, and had photographs taken to prove we had done our duty.

'A smart way of being remembered for ever,' said Pete, 'I must remember to ask folk to do the same to me after I've gone.'

'Why wait,' muttered Mitch, 'we'll oblige here and now.'

A small girl and her parents appeared in the gateway, the child carrying a lamb draped in a blue sheet with a red ribbon round its neck. Mzia asked why they were bringing the lamb to the monastery and was told that the little girl had been cured of an illness through the power of prayer. They had brought the lamb as a thanksgiving offering to the clergy who had prayed for her.

Exit Nimrod!

Back in Tbilisi, Pete had received a message from his firm summoning him back to London. In typical bullish terms, he told us that something had come up that only he could deal with, but that he would return to Georgia soon.

'I certainly hope he comes back to do the decent thing by one of those lovely girls he fooled around with,' mused the ever vigilant Frank.

But Pete didn't return. We got vague messages from him that said a lot but told us very little, and then the messages ceased. Whatever his faults, I missed him, his lovely, clever girlfriends and even his 'sermons' almost as much as we all missed our fascinating excursions in the four-wheel drive.

Chapter 11

'Parting is such Sweet Sorrow'

'We are so sorry to be saying goodbye,' Tamuna was on her feet proposing a toast to us at our farewell supra. 'Soso wanted to be here to thank you, and to toast you in best Georgian fashion but he has been called away on business with the Minister'.

Well, there's a surprise!' murmured Mitch, and then asked, 'We were to send our final report to Soso and to discuss it with him. Can you arrange that before we leave, Tamuna? We must do that to honour our contract.'

We all knew what Mitch was up to, but we kept a straight face.

'You can all send your final reports to me,' said Tamuna brightly, 'I will pass them on to Soso. If he wants to discuss them with you he will say.'

'Don't hold your breath,' whispered Mitch, 'I tell you, the guy doesn't exist!' And indeed we left without ever getting to the bottom of the Soso mystery, but exist or not, throughout our stay his 'virtual presence' was unfailingly useful to Tamuna and our Georgian colleagues. Frank remained convinced that he did exist if not now, somewhere, sometime – 'or why else would he have a bathroom in the Ministry?' he would muse. This piece of hard evidence notwithstanding, throughout our stay Soso remained an absent conundrum but yet an ever present force to be reckoned with.

As Frank, Mitch and I gazed round that final supra table, we all knew we would miss Georgia and our Georgian colleagues very much. From the moment we arrived in Georgia we had all fallen under its spell, and our experience of working there was to prove unforgettable for all the right reasons.

What were the reasons? The country is beautiful of course, has a fascinating history, holds exquisite treasures, and its food and wine are literally incomparable. But it is the Georgian people that we all fell for in a big way. Their friendship, unstinting hospitality, and unique way of doing things and making progress in their own time-honoured fashion won our admiration, respect and love. We had all worked hard as a team and in the end had helped improve some things that badly needed attention and, for others, we had set out some promising directions that should help towards useful improvements in the longer term. Whatever we had achieved together had been done in such a relaxed atmosphere and with such a willing acceptance of one another's view of the world as to leave a lasting mark on all of us, Georgians and newcomers alike.

Questions remain! Will our hard-working Georgian friends ever succumb to keeping minutes of meetings? To drawing up agendas? To using wretched flip charts and PowerPoint presentations? I suppose, sadly, they will! Will they take on board all the EU regulations and other notions current in the West which will make them ever more like us? I suppose, sadly, they will!

But perhaps they will beat us at our own game for they have learnt a thing or two over the millennia about surviving with their unique way of doing things intact. They are beset by challenges on so many fronts: ...somehow stabilising their democratic political structures and making them work Georgian-style; steadily reinvigorating an economy which imploded on the collapse of the Soviet system; resisting 'friends' from the West bearing 'gifts', some of which they want and some they would be better without; neighbours who all too often wish them ill; disaffected regions, some of which have already broken away, some under foreign pressure to do so, some that have returned but in a half-hearted manner; refugees who have lost everything fleeing from these regions; poverty manifest in the streets of Tbilisi, especially among the very old who must already have endured unimaginable suffering over the course of the twentieth century; young people highly educated, cultured and articulate but with jobs unmatched to their skills and abilities, or with no jobs at all,

And yet all these challenges are faced by all we met with such optimism, such dedication, such vitality, such vision for the future of Georgia and its people as to put us in the West to shame. Georgians will now accomplish much, but they will do it in their own way and on their own terms. That was Mitch's final toast to our Georgian friends, with Frank and I in full agreement.

As we walked back to our hotel, we all three reflected on the changes for the better we had seen during our stay: pavements and parks repaired, new shops opening everywhere, people with more money to spend on their clothes and their homes, bustling restaurants, young people enjoying café culture, international exhibitions and shows arriving in the cities; Tbilisi's beautiful old houses and verandas in the Old City being tastefully restored.

'If only they could now sort things out with the Russians and do something about their bloody roads,' mused Mitch, 'this place would be awash with tourists in no time.'

'Well thank goodness we have seen it before the tourist descends on it,' said Frank.

'Of all the memories and experiences you have both had here, which will you treasure most?' I asked my two friends when we were having a final nightcap back in the hotel.

They both thought for a while. Frank said:

'It is the revival of religion here in Georgia. Whether you are religious or not, weren't you amazed by the religious zeal in Georgia? From the time they became a Christian country, they have been invaded by nearly everybody you can imagine, but the Georgian church has survived it all, and we have seen their churches packed with people, young and old, and their monasteries and seminaries reopened. Have you not been amazed that the first thing to be restored and reopened in so many of their town and villages is the church, even before they have running water, electricity or made any other improvements to their homes? It has proved to me the power of spirituality that exists in all of us which seems to be as necessary to our existence as the air we breathe. But you are both looking at me very sceptically, so what do you think?'

'Might religion not just have a certain novelty value for them?' asked Mitch. 'They were denied religion for sixty plus years under the Communists so they are now packing the churches again. Might the novelty soon wear off?'

'I don't know which of you is right,' I said,' but back in Northern Ireland there is a close connection between your religion and the nation you want to belong to. I detect the same here. Showing you are Orthodox is your badge for telling the world you are pleased and proud to be Georgian too. It could be as much about nationalism as about religion, spirituality or the novelty value of religious freedom.'

Nothing daunted by our scepticism, Frank continued:

'Well, whatever the reason, I take away two memories. The first is the vision of the little Orthodox nuns carrying the icon in procession round the church at Bodbe where St Nino is buried. You remember we visited the church when we were on our way back from working in east Georgia. The other was when we saw the beautiful fresco of the Angel Gabriel at the church at Atenis Sioni. Remember the problems we had finding the guy who had the key to the church, and when we did track him down he broke all the rules and allowed us to climb the scaffolding to see the restoration work on the frescoes. So the devotion of the young nuns at Bodbe, and the painstaking restoration of the Gabriel and the other frescos at Atenis Sioni said it all for me. Christian spirituality will survive no matter what. I think I needed to come to Georgia to fully realise that, especially with the state of our world at present,' and he took a long sip of his Coke.

'Well you two are very silent!' he continued, glaring at us. 'Now Mitch, come clean! What will you treasure most from your time here?' Mitch's answer surprised us both. 'Birdsong,' he said simply. Didn't you both notice that everywhere we went the Georgian countryside is bathed in birdsong. It just proves to me that in the West we must indeed be killing our birds with darn pesticides on a grand scale just as the conservationists keep telling us. Here the air is pure, the water is pure, the crops are largely fertiliser-free, and so the birds flourish. Of course, like you I have enjoyed greatly the warmth of the friendships which we have all experienced, the unspoiled beauty of Tbilisi, the generous hospitality – all that too, but my abiding memory of Georgia will be the birdsong.' He paused and looked away for a few minutes, and I think at that moment Frank and I both realised that we scarcely knew Mitch at all.

'And now what about you?' said Frank. 'It was you who posed the question, and got us both to bear our souls. What is your abiding memory?'

'I will write a book about it,' I said, 'and if it ever gets published I'll send you both a copy. Then you'll know!'

Chapter 12

... and finally! Let's all Supra!

Throughout our stay in Georgia it can fairly be said that all three of us ate to excess, and steadily grew in size in all the wrong places. The temptation to gorge on Georgian food was irresistible for, as I hope this account has repeatedly made clear, it is, quite simply, delicious!

We left thinking that the magnificent Georgian institution, the supra, is something the whole world would do well to embrace. For though it may play havoc with the waistline, its power to break down barriers and establish firm friendships matches and often outshines even an Irish evening's 'craic'. The supra is all inclusive: the dishes come thick and fast, the rich wine flows in abundance, the toasts embrace all shades of opinion, and the feeling of well-being and fellowship around a supra table must soften all but the hardest heart. Even the abstemious Frank came to appreciate its 'healing and settling' quality, as he put it, while never once departing from his strongly held principles about excesses of food and drink.

The mystery which continued to baffle us throughout our stay was why the Georgian cuisine, which is the centre piece of the supra, is not better known in the West? Nana had remarked at the famous Christmas supra feast in Andreo and Manana's home 'If only we Georgians had got to the USA before the Italians, it would have been our Khachapuri that would have taken the world by storm and not their pizzas!'.

When our Georgian colleagues saw how much we enjoyed the variety of Georgian dishes and the quality of Georgian wines, they would exhort us to 'spread the word in the West! Visitors like you must tell the world about our khachapuri, khinkali and all our other Georgian dishes.'

As with so much else, Georgia now wants to share its remarkable cuisine with all of us, and that is my sole mission in this chapter! To offer you a guide on how to cook just some of Georgia's delicious dishes. I can do no less! Did I not introduce the Georgians to the delights of Irish whiskey on my very first evening! And if the sample of dishes I include here are accompanied by Georgia's superb wines – Tsinandali, the pride of Georgian whites, or the highly acclaimed rich red Mukuzani – the victory of the Georgian kitchen over Western palates will surely be complete.

Some of the dishes we enjoyed

These recipes are taken from Professor Darra Goldstein's excellent book *The Georgian Feast: the Vibrant Culture and Savory Food of the Republic of Georgia* published by the University of California Press in 1999. Professor Goldstein provides us with an easy-to-follow step-by-step guide to the full range of delicacies that is the Georgian cuisine. The sample I have taken from this highly acclaimed award-winning publication is only a taster of the Georgian culinary delights the book has to offer.

BREAD

Khachapuri, Georgian cheese bread, accompanies almost every meal in Georgia, and so takes pride of place on any Georgian menu. Khachapuri comes in many guises, and here is a version of it that we enjoyed.

Khachapuri Cheese Bread – The Classic Golden Yeast Version. Serves 8-12.

Ingredients:
¾ cup of milk
1 ½ packs (4 ½ teaspoons) active dry yeast.
½ teaspoon honey

6 tablespoons butter at room temperature.

¼ teaspoon ground coriander seed.

1 ¾ teaspoons salt.

2 cups unbleached white flour.

1 lb. Muenster cheese.

½ lb. processed cheese.

3 eggs.

1 tablespoon melted butter.

Directions:

1. Heat the milk to lukewarm.
2. Dissolve the yeast and honey in ¼ cup of the milk, and set aside for 10 minutes.
3. Stir in the remaining milk.
4. Add the room temperature butter, the ground coriander seed, 1½ teaspoons salt and the flour.
5. Mix well.
6. Turn the dough out onto a floured board and knead for 10 minutes until smooth and elastic.
7. Place in a greased bowl, turning the dough to grease the top.
8. Cover and allow to rise in a warm place until it doubles in bulk (1 ½ to 2 hours).

Preparing the filling:

1. Grate the Muenster cheese.
2. Cream the processed cheese in a medium sized bowl.
3. Stir in the grated Muenster until well blended.
4. Beat the eggs and stir into the cheese mixture together with the remaining ¼ teaspoon salt.
5. Beat until smooth and light.
6. Set aside.

When the dough has doubled in bulk:

1. Punch it down and then let it rise again until doubled (about 45 minutes).

2. Punch down once more and divide into 3 equal pieces.
3. On a floured board, roll each piece of dough into a circle about 12 inches in diameter.
4. Grease three 8-inch cake tins or pie pans and centre a round of dough in each pan.
5. Divide the cheese mixture into 3 equal parts.
6. Place 1/3 of the filling in each circle of dough, heaping it in the centre.
7. Fold the edges of the dough in towards the centre, working clockwise and allowing each fold of dough to overlap the previous one, until the cheese mixture is completely enclosed in the pleated dough.
8. Grasp the excess dough in the centre of the bread and twist in into a knot to seal.

Preheat the oven to 190 degrees C/gas 5.
1. Let the bread stand for 10 minutes.
2. Brush with the melted butter.
3. Bake for about 45 minutes or until browned.
4. Take the khachapuri out of the pans.
5. Serve hot or at room temperatures.

The Ajaruli Variation

Another interesting variation of Khachapuri is Ajaruli. It comes highly recommended by Mitch who sampled it when he thought it best to cut his losses and take cover in a restaurant on the shores of the Black Sea. Ajaruli can best be described as a 'bread boat' with an egg floating on its deck of pastry, butter and cheese.

Kartopiliani – Potato Bread

Ireland prides itself on its potato bread and Georgia too has its own distinct version – Kartopiliani – which is well worth trying.

Makes two large portions enough to serve 10.

Ingredients:

Bread:

2 eggs.

2 cups sour cream.

4 cups unbleached white flour.

10 tablespoons softened butter.

1 teaspoon baking soda divided into 4 parts.

Filling:

4 lbs. potatoes.

1 tablespoon salt.

4 medium sized peeled onions.

¾ cup vegetable oil.

1 teaspoon freshly ground black pepper.

Directions:

1. Cream the butter and beat in the eggs and sour cream.
2. Mix in the flour to make a soft dough.
3. On a floured board, roll the dough to a 15 by 18 inch rectangle.
4. Sprinkle with ¼ teaspoon of the baking soda.
5. Fold the dough in half, then in half again, and roll out once more to a 15 by 18 inch rectangle.
6. Sprinkle with ¼ teaspoon of the remaining baking soda.
7. Repeat the folding process.
8. Repeat this process 4 times until all the baking soda has been incorporated into the dough.
9. After folding the dough the last time place it in a floured bowl, cover it, and leave it to rise for 6 to 8 hours at room temperature until doubled in bulk. Don't let the dough sit any longer or it will sour.

To make the filling:

1. Boil the potatoes until soft.
2. Peel and mash them well.
3. Dice the onions and sauté in the oil until soft.

4. Stir them into the mashed potatoes along with the salt and pepper.
5. Divide the potatoes mixture in half and set aside.

Preheat the oven to 180 degrees C/Gas 4..

When the dough has risen:
1 Divide it into 2 parts.
2. On a lightly floured sheet, roll one part of the dough into a 10 by 18 inch rectangle.
3. Spread half the potato mixture over half of the dough and fold the other half over it to cover.
4. Seal the bread by bringing the lower edges up over the top of the dough to form a rim.
5. Make another portion of the bread with the remaining dough.
6. Brush the breads with beaten egg yolk and bake for 40 to 45 minutes until well browned.
7. Serve warm.

SAUCES

Georgian cookery abounds in a great variety of sauces. These accompany almost everything – poultry, meat, fish, vegetables – and are so tasty some are served on their own with only bread to mop them up. Here are just two to try from the great range available.

Tkemali – Plum Sauce

Makes 1 pint.

Ingredients:
1½ lbs. plums [not too sweet or ripe.]
¼ cup water.
¾ teaspoon whole coriander seeds.
1 teaspoon fennel seeds.

2 large garlic cloves, peeled and roughly chopped.
1 teaspoon cayenne pepper.
½ teaspoon salt.
1 tablespoon finely chopped fresh mint.
One third cup finely chopped coriander.

Directions:
1. Cut the plums in half and remove the stones.
2. Place in a saucepan with the water and bring to the boil.
3. Simmer, covered, for 15 minutes, or until soft.
4. In a mortar and pestle, pound together the coriander seed, fennel seed, garlic, cayenne, and salt to make a fine paste.
5. When the plums are soft, put them through a sieve and return to a clean pan. Bring to the boil and cook over medium heat, stirring, for 3 minutes.
6. Stir in the ground spices and continue cooking until the mixture thickens slightly, for about 5 minutes.
7. Stir in the chopped mint and coriander and remove from the heat.
8. Pour into a jar while still hot. Either cool at room temperature and in the fridge.
9. Store in a sealed jar between use.

Makvali – Blackberry Sauce

Ingredients:
1½ cups ripe blackberries.
1 peeled and roughly chopped small garlic clove.
¼ teaspoon salt.
½ small hot red or green pepper, chopped.
¼ cup finely chopped fresh dill and coriander.
1 or 2 teaspoons lemon juice.

1. Force the blackberries through a fine sieve into a bowl.
2. In a mortar and pestle, pound the garlic, salt, and hot pepper into a paste and add to the sieved blackberries.

3. Stir in the chopped herbs and lemon juice to taste.
4. Serve at room temperature.

SOUPS

Georgian soups can be quite exotic, for example, kharcho which is made from stale bread and yogurt or can just be a simple dish easy to prepare. The soup Mitch, Frank and I enjoyed most was Chikhirtma and here it is.

Chikhirtma – Lemon chicken soup

Serves 6.

Ingredients:
One 3-lb. chicken (including the giblets except for the liver).
1 large peeled onion.
2 peeled garlic cloves.
½ teaspoon whole black peppercorns.
4 sprigs coriander.
6 cups cold water.
2 tablespoons butter.
2 onions, peeled and finely chopped.
1 tablespoon flour.
½ teaspoon powdered saffron.
Heaped ½ teaspoon ground cinnamon.
½ teaspoon ground coriander seed.
¾ teaspoon salt.
Freshly ground black pepper.
2 eggs.
½ cup freshly squeezed lemon juice.
Chopped coriander, basil, or dill for garnish

Directions:
1. Bring the chicken, onion, garlic, peppercorns, and coriander to the boil in a large saucepan, skimming any foam that rises to the surface.

2. Reduce heat and simmer the chicken in the broth for 2 ½ hours.
3. Strain the broth and retain. [At this stage the chicken meat can be removed from the bones.]
4. In a large saucepan, melt the butter and sauté the chopped onion until golden.
5. Sprinkle the flour over the onion and cook for 1 minute, stirring.
6. Add the saffron, cinnamon, coriander, salt, and pepper and mix well.
7. Slowly pour in the reserved chicken stock.
8. In a separate bowl, beat the eggs well and stir in the lemon juice.
9. Slowly stir in about 2 cups of the hot broth.
10. Pour the egg mixture back into the soup, stirring constantly.
11. Simmer very gently for 1 minute to thicken slightly. Do not allow the soup to boil.
12. Serve garnished with chopped coriander, basil, or dill.

MEAT DISHES

Of all the unusual dishes I have ever tasted anywhere, the Georgian Khinkali must take pride of place. It is a real find, and greatly enhanced by the skill you have to acquire to eat it! You hold the 'purse' by its doughy top 'knot' above your mouth, bite a small hole in the purse and catch the meat filling in your mouth. If you try it any other way, you will miss the rich juices draining from the purse. Don't eat the top knot; instead let the knots accumulate on your plate to help you calculate how many purses you have eaten. I predict you too will find Khinkali compulsive!

Here are two versions.

Khinkali – Dumplings or 'purses' of spicy meat.

Makes 25 Khinkali Dumplings

Ingredients:
4 cups unbleached white flour.
1¼ teaspoons salt.
1¼ cups warm water.
1 lb. mixed ground beef and pork.
½ teaspoon freshly ground black pepper.
1¼ teaspoons salt.
Pinch of cayenne.
¼ teaspoon ground caraway seed.
3 small peeled onions.
½ cup warm water or vegetable or beef bouillon.

Directions:
1. Make a firm dough by combining the flour, salt and warm water. Knead for 5 minutes, then let sit, covered, for 30 to 40 minutes.
2. Meanwhile make the filling. Mix the ground meats and spices. Finely chop the onions and stir them into the meat mixture. With your hands, knead in the water or bouillon.
3. Divide the dough into 25 pieces.
4. On a floured board, roll each piece out to a 6 inch round.
5. Place about 2 tablespoons of filling in the centre of each round.

Nos. 6 – 8 below take a little practice!

6. Make accordion pleats all the way round the filling by folding the edges of the dough in towards the centre.
7. Move in a clockwise direction, allowing each fold of dough to overlap the previous one, until the filling is completely enclosed in the pleated dough.
8. Holding the dumpling firmly in one hand, twist the pleats together at the centre to seal, breaking off the excess dough at the topknot.

9. Cook the dumplings in salted, boiling water for 12 to 15 minutes.
10. Serve hot.

An alternative to meat-filled khinkali is a plain cheese (e.g. Cheddar) filling.

Ingredients:
1 lb. plain cheese.
1 teaspoon salt.
Freshly ground black pepper.
2 eggs.

Directions:
1. Press the cheese through a sieve into a bowl.
2. Beat in the salt, pepper and eggs, mixing well.
3. Proceed as directed above.

Now for another compelling Georgian meat dish with a memorable and amusing name!

Chizhi-Pizhi – Georgian Meatloaf

Serves 2 to 4.

Ingredients:
1 small peeled and chopped onion.
1 large peeled and chopped garlic clove.
2 tablespoons butter.
1 lb. lean ground beef or lamb.
¾ teaspoon salt.
Freshly ground black pepper.
¼ cup chopped mixed fresh dill and parsley.
Pinch of salt.
2 beaten eggs.

Directions:
1. Preheat the oven to 180 degrees F or gas 4.
2. Grease two shallow 6-inch casseroles.
3. Lightly sauté the onion and garlic in the butter, then mix the ground meat along with the salt and pepper to taste.
4. Divide the mixture and press it into the prepared dishes.
5. Whisk the chopped herbs and pinch of salt into the beaten eggs.
6. Pour the eggs over the meat mixture.
7. Bake for 30 minutes

CHEESE AND EGGS DISHES

As we travelled around Georgia, we constantly marvelled at its fertile farm land. It was clear that agriculture is now re-establishing itself as one of the country's main assets after years of labouring under the communist command economy. One very practical outcome is the quality of its dairy produce, and we quickly came to appreciate the great variety of its cheese, yogurts and egg dishes. Here is a dish we constantly returned to, and which displays the Georgians' inventiveness with delicious combinations accompanying its unique Suluguni cheese.

Note: Suluguni is a popular Georgian cheese but Mozzarella is a suitable substitute if Suluguni is not available.

Gadazelili Khveli - Cooked Cheese with Mint.

Serves 6.

Ingredients:
1 cup whole milk.
1 lb. mozzarella cut into chunks.
½ teaspoon salt.
2 tablespoons chopped fresh mint.

Directions:
1. Bring milk to the boil.
2. Add the cheese and stir for about 2 minutes, until the cheese melts.
3. Transfer the cheese to a plate, keeping the milk simmering.
4. Work the salt into the cheese.
5. To mix the mint, fold the cheese until the mint is evenly distributed.
6. Form the cheese into one or more balls and return it to the simmering milk.
7. Heat gently for a few minutes more, then turn out the cheese and the milk together in a bowl.
8. Serve warm or at room temperature.

POULTRY

I confess I am not a great poultry lover, but that quickly changed when Georgia's poultry dishes were accompanied – as they usually were – by tangy sauces and other imaginative ingredients. But even without these accompaniments, the poultry dishes really did taste better, and my American friends attributed this to the fact that the chickens, ducks, turkeys and other poultry range freely just as nature intended. Whatever the reason, Georgian poultry dishes enriched our lives, and here is one we returned to many times.

Katmis Bazhe – Chicken in Bazhe [walnut] Sauce.

Serves 6

Preparing the Bazhe Sauce:
Ingredients:
1 ½ cups walnuts.
5 peeled and roughly chopped garlic cloves.
¾ cup boiling water.
2 teaspoons red wine vinegar.
½ teaspoon salt.

1 teaspoon ground marigold bouillon.

¾ teaspoon ground coriander seeds.

¼ teaspoon paprika.

Dash of cayenne.

Directions:

1. Chop the nuts coarsely in a food processor.
2. Add the garlic and continue to grind to a paste.
3. Transfer to a bowl and beat in the boiling water, stirring constantly until smooth.
4. Stir in the wine vinegar and spices.
5. Allow to sit for several hours.

Other ingredients:

One 4-to 5-lb. roasting chicken.

Butter or olive oil.

Half an hour before serving:

1. Rub the chicken skin with the butter or olive oil.
2. Place in a shallow pan and roast at 190 degrees C or gas 5 for 1 to 1 ¼ hours basting occasionally.
3. Remove the chicken from the oven and allow to sit for 10 minutes before carving.
4. Pour the bazhe sauce over slices of the hot roast chicken.

FISH DISHES

Fish dishes are a special favourite of mine, and at these Georgian cuisine really excels. Fish was often served very simply just out of the oven with few embellishments but more often it arrived with walnut, plums or pomegranate sauce or in a delightful herb stew. Here is one of my favourite fish dishes.

Tevzi Brotseulis Tsvenshi –
Cold Fish with Pomegranate and Walnut Sauce

Serves 3 to 4

Ingredients:
1¼ lbs. of sea bass, whitefish or red snapper.
Salt.
Freshly ground black pepper.
2 tablespoons white flour.
3 tablespoons vegetable oil.
2 medium peeled & chopped onions.
1 tablespoon butter.
½ cup shelled walnuts.
1 large garlic peeled clove.
1 tablespoon chopped hot red or green pepper.
½ cup water.
½ cup unsweetened pomegranate juice.
2 tablespoons tomato paste.

Directions:
1. Sprinkle the fish with salt and pepper.
2. Dust both sides with flour.
3. Heat the oil in a large frying pan.
4. Fry the fish, turning once, for 10 to 20 minutes, depending on the thickness of the fillet, until it is crusty and brown.
5. Sauté the onions in the butter over a medium heat until golden, for about 10 minutes.
6. Transfer the fish to a shallow flameproof casserole.
7. Spread the cooked onions over it.

The sauce:
1. Grind the walnuts with the garlic and ½ teaspoon salt.
2. Stir in the hot pepper, water, pomegranate juice, and tomato paste, mixing well.
3. Pour the sauce over the fish and bring to the boil.

4. Simmer, covered, for 2 minutes.
5. Remove from the heat and allow to cool.
6. Store in the fridge.
7. Serve chilled with twisted orange slices as a garnish.

SIDE DISHES

Side dishes of great variety quite literally adorn the Georgian table and are often a meal in themselves. The Georgian's ability to make rather lacklustre ingredients – cabbage, beans, spinach – excite the gastric juices is amply demonstrated in these examples.

Charkhlis Chogi – Beets with Cherry Sauce

Serve 2 to 3.

Ingredients:
1lb. beets.
1 medium peeled and chopped onion.
1 tablespoon butter.
1/3 cup tart dried cherries.
10 tablespoons water.
2 tablespoons chopped parsley.
2 tablespoons chopped coriander or dill.
1/8 teaspoon salt.

Directions:
1. Preheat the oven to 190 degrees C or gas 5.
2. Scrub the beets but do not peel.
3. Bake until tender for 1 to 1 ½ hours.
4. Meanwhile sauté the onion in the butter until soft for 10 to 15 minutes.
5. Simmer the cherries in the water until very soft for about 15 minutes.
6. Force through a sieve, adding additional water, if necessary, to make ¼ cup of thick sauce.

7. When the beets are ready, peel and slice them thinly.
8. Place in a bowl and add the cooked onion and cherry sauce.
9. Stir in the chopped herbs and salt.
10. Serve the same day if possible.

Kombostos Ruleti Nigvzit – Cabbage with Walnuts.

Serves 6 to 8.

Ingredients:
1 small head white cabbage.
3 heaped cups shelled walnuts.
¾ teaspoon whole coriander seed.
¾ teaspoon ground marigold bouillon.
1 ½ teaspoons salt.
4 small garlic cloves, peeled and roughly chopped.
3 sprigs coriander.
Pinch of cayenne.
Pinch of the dried fenugreek herb.
1 tablespoon red wine vinegar.
6 tablespoons mixed chopped fresh herbs (parsley, coriander, dill, celery leaf).
Pomegranate seeds.

Directions:
1. Core the cabbage and cook in a large saucepan of boiling water until the leaves are tender (about 25 minutes).
2. Drain well.

To prepare the filling:
1. Chop the walnuts very fine.
2. In a mortar and pestle, pound into a paste the coriander seed, marigold, salt, garlic, coriander, and a pinch each of cayenne and the fenugreek herb.
3. Stir into the walnuts.

4. Add the vinegar.
5. Stir in the mixed chopped herbs.
6. Mix well.

To assemble:
1. Carefully separate the head of cabbage into leaves.
2. Working with one leaf at a time, cut out the tough rib.
3. Mound about one tablespoon of the walnut filling in the centre of the leaf and roll it up to make a packet.
4. Repeat with the remaining leaves.
5. Cut each cabbage roll in half on the diagonal to reveal the filling.
6. Serve at room temperature, garnished with pomegranate seeds.

Ispanakhi Matsvnit – Spinach with Yogurt.

Serves 4

Ingredients:
1 lb. spinach.
2 leafy sprigs coriander.
1 garlic clove, peeled and roughly chopped.
Pinch of salt.
1 cup plain yogurt.

Directions:
1. Wash the spinach well and cook it, covered, for 5 minutes.
2. Drain thoroughly.
3. Squeeze out any excess moisture and then mince.
4. In a mortar and pestle, pound together the coriander, garlic, and salt and add them to the yogurt.
5. Beat the mixture well and stir in the spinach.
6. Serve chilled.

SWEETS

Frank has a sweet tooth, and so he was in his element at the Georgian table. Since our hosts, and indeed Georgian restaurants, tended to bring the whole range of dishes to the table at much the same time, Frank would launch himself at the sweets long before the rest of us. We soon learnt to grab our share and hoard it as best we could until we had reached that stage of the meal. Mitch and I were a little more discriminating than Frank over the sweet courses and usually plumped for the following - in so far as we could manage the sweet courses at all!

Gozinaki – Honey Coated Walnuts

Serves 20 – 25

Ingredients:
1 lb walnuts.
1 cup honey.

Directions:
1. Chop walnuts carefully taking care not to break pieces.
2. Toast walnuts until light gold.
3. In a big saucepan bring honey to the boil, add sugar, stir slowly until honey gets darker.
4. Add walnuts to the pan and stir slowly for 10 minutes.
5. Wet the wooden board and spread the mixture well until ½ an inch thick.
6. Cut into squares and diamonds, place on the plate with the upper side down and store in the fridge.

These are just some of the dishes that should help to get a good supra underway anywhere!

Among the vast treasury of good things I gained from my time in Georgia, perhaps the supra, with its spirit of well-being and companionship captures for me the essence of Georgia and the Georgians – their generosity, warm heartedness, creativity, and relaxed approach to life.

There, at the other end of Europe, in this jewel in the Caucasus, I so very often heard echoes also of the best of 'things Irish,' and was reminded constantly of the approach to life and to the stranger that warm hearted people the world over share, and is surely best reflected in the Georgian poet Rustaveli's words:

'A guest is a gift from God.'